CITIES OF ROMA

CITY OF LONDON SCHOOL

NAME	FORM	DATE

Classical World Series

Aristophanes and his Theatre of the Absurd, Paul Cartledge
Art and the Romans, Anne Haward
Athens and Sparta, S. Todd
Athens under the Tyrants, J. Smith
Athletics in the Ancient World, Zahra Newby
Attic Orators, Michael Edwards
Augustan Rome, Andrew Wallace-Hadrill
Cicero and the End of the Roman Republic, Thomas Wiedemann
Classical Archaeology in the Field, S.J. Hill, L. Bowkett and
    K. & D. Wardle
Classical Epic: Homer and Virgil, Richard Jenkyns
Democracy in Classical Athens, Christopher Carey
Early Greek Lawgivers, John Lewis
Environment and the Classical World, Patricia Jeskins
Greece and the Persians, John Sharwood Smith
Greek and Roman Historians, Timothy E. Duff
Greek and Roman Medicine, Helen King
Greek Architecture, R. Tomlinson
Greek Literature in the Roman Empire, Jason König
Greek Tragedy: An Introduction, Marion Baldock
Greek Vases, Elizabeth Moignard
Julio-Claudian Emperors, T. Wiedemann
Lucretius and the Didactic Epic, Monica Gale
Morals and Values in Ancient Greece, John Ferguson
Mycenaean World, K. & D. Wardle
Plato's Republic and the Greek Enlightenment, Hugh Lawson-Tancred
Plays of Euripides, James Morwood
Plays of Sophocles, A.F. Garvie
Political Life in the City of Rome, J.R. Patterson
Religion and the Greeks, Robert Garland
Religion and the Romans, Ken Dowden
Roman Architecture, Martin Thorpe
Roman Britain, S.J. Hill and S. Ireland
Roman Frontiers in Britain, David Breeze
Roman Satirists and Their Masks, Susanna Braund
Slavery in Classical Greece, N. Fisher
Women in Classical Athens, Sue Blundell

Classical World Series

CITIES OF ROMAN ITALY

Pompeii, Herculaneum and Ostia

Guy de la Bédoyère

Bristol Classical Press

First published in 2010 by
Bristol Classical Press, an imprint of
Gerald Duckworth & Co. Ltd.
90-93 Cowcross Street, London EC1M 6BF
Tel: 020 7490 7300
Fax: 020 7490 0080
info@duckworth-publishers.co.uk
www.ducknet.co.uk

A catalogue record for this book is available
from the British Library

ISBN 978 1 85399 728 0

Typeset by Ray Davies
Printed and bound in Great Britain by
CPI Antony Rowe, Chippenham & Eastbourne

Contents

Preface

Three Italian cities dominate studies of the Roman world: Pompeii and Herculaneum, suspended by the destructive force of Mount Vesuvius in AD 79, and the picturesque ruins of Ostia Antica, Rome's ancient port. They provide unique glimpses of the environments in which Roman society flourished and played out its everyday dramas. No wonder then that they form the backbone to some of the papers in today's Classical Studies courses. However, while books on Pompeii are abundant, the other two cities are nothing like as well served for an English-speaking or non-specialist readership. This book has been written to provide a starting point for those studies, by integrating all three sites into a discussion that covers general aspects of Roman city life as well as selected individual buildings.

The three towns were very different places. Pompeii and Herculaneum were two southern Italian cities with their origins in Greek and Samnite culture. They were dominated by local landowners and freedmen and their histories as cities end in AD 79. Ostia was the port of Rome, lived in and frequented by international traders, imperial officials, and artisans. Its climax came in the second century AD and it remained of importance until the fourth century when it fell into gradual decline.

In general, Latin terms and their English equivalents or translations are supplied. Important words or phrases from significant inscriptions and literary sources are also included in Latin as well as English. This is unnecessary for most students but will be of use to those who are also studying Latin. Translations are generally widely available, especially in the invaluable Cooley and Cooley sourcebook for Pompeii, but it is always worth remembering that translations often paraphrase the original meaning or blur subtleties in the original wording.

It has not been possible, for space reasons, to include as many illustrations as I would have liked. However, there are now so many on-line resources available (see p. 117-18) that I hope the reader will forgive this. All photographs are by myself and were taken between 2006 and 2009.

Visits to these sites are of inestimable value to teachers and students alike, but at the time of writing increasing problems of money, vandalism, and deterioration have led to dramatic levels of closures. Many of the key buildings are no longer readily accessible and special arrangements for access must be made.

I would like to thank Dr Roger Rees of St Andrews University and Bristol Classical Press for his enthusiastic reception of my suggestion of this title and for fielding it through the commissioning process, Professor Roger Ling of Manchester University for his meticulous and detailed comments on the text, Dr Jo Berry of Swansea University for her generous help and advice with numerous queries, especially tracking down publications of the house of Aulus Umbricius Scaurus, and for commenting on the text, the Soprintendenza and staff of the archaeological sites of Pompeii and Herculaneum for arranging access to key buildings, Sarah Court of the Herculaneum Conservation Project for her invaluable help on-site in securing access to Herculaneum's key buildings, Lucy Harrow, principal examiner for the OCR examination board's CC6 (Cities of Roman Italy) paper for welcoming the book and her advice and suggestions, my A-Level students at Kesteven and Sleaford High School (especially Florence Smith-Nicholls) for test-driving the text while studying, and my wife Rosemary for enduring gruelling days at Ostia, Pompeii and Herculaneum during the research for the book. Some of these have been kind enough to point out my mistakes, but any that remain are, of course, my responsibility alone.

Guy de la Bédoyère, Sleaford 2009

Chapter 1

Background to the Cities: History and Development

Rome's emergence as the supreme power in Italy was the product of centuries of warfare. By the end of the fourth century BC she had defeated not only the combined forces of the Latin League but also the Etruscans. A series of wars against the Appennine Samnite peoples finally concluded in 290 BC when the Samnites were forced to accept the status of Roman allies. Defeats of the Greek cities of the south followed, leaving Rome in control of the Italian peninsula by 272 BC.

Ostia

As Rome's port Ostia was in a different league to Pompeii and Herculaneum, which were small Italian cities where most of the elite were local landowners and wealthy freedmen. Conversely, at Ostia imperial officials and international merchants lived and worked alongside local freedmen and artisans in a major trading centre at the heart of the Roman Empire.

Around the middle of the fourth century BC a fort was established at the mouth of the Tiber. Indeed, Ostia's name comes from the Latin *ostium*, 'mouth'. The strategic importance to Rome, then becoming the most powerful force in Italy, is obvious. By 267 BC Ostia, now a town in its own right, was important enough for Rome to appoint a prefect of the fleet there. Ostia began to play a major role in Roman history as a port for imported goods which were brought up the Tiber to Rome or taken by road. In 217 BC during the Second Punic War supplies were shipped out from Ostia for the Roman army fighting the Carthaginian general Hannibal in Spain. Ostia continued to play a major role during the war, its inhabitants being exempted from military service so that they could service the port facilities. In 204 BC, with Rome desperate for any source of sustenance, a stone representing the eastern mother goddess Cybele was brought to Ostia from Phrygia to fulfil a prophecy that Rome could avert catastrophe with her help. In 87 BC Ostia was sacked by the general Marius in his civil war against Sulla. After this Ostia was rebuilt and fortified. As Rome grew in power, so did Ostia, beginning gradually to rival Pozzuoli's (ancient Puteoli) role as Rome's principal commercial port of entry.

But Ostia had a problem. The Tiber was narrow at Ostia (around 100 metres) and it was silting up. This became increasingly serious as Rome's demands grew. By the mid-first century BC it had become clear that something would have to be done. Small and medium-sized ships could enter and be towed upriver to Rome, but the largest merchant ships were forced to ride at anchor out at sea and be offloaded by smaller vessels. This was potentially disastrous in winter, a season that shippers avoided at all costs if they could. The only other option was, according to Strabo (v.3.5; see Selected Texts), for ships to be part-unloaded at sea so that they could navigate upriver to Rome without fear of running aground on the shallow riverbed. Plutarch (*Caesar* 58.10) records that Julius Caesar planned various works, including breakwaters and clearage of obstructions, to reduce the risk to shipping coming in to Ostia, as well as to build a new harbour, but none of these was ever executed by him.

Consolidating the new Roman imperial state was far more of a priority to Augustus, though he did organize the grain supply (*annona*) under the command of its own dedicated prefect. Ostia had to wait for Claudius (AD 41-54). Claudius was acutely conscious of his reputation as the family idiot and stooge for the Praetorian Guard in Rome. He identified, correctly, that fulfilling the thwarted ambitions of his most famous forbear, Julius Caesar, might go a long way to remedying his status and public image. Invading Britain was one of the schemes he adopted. One of the others was Ostia. Claudius had also been faced with the prospect of food riots when supplies of the corn dole ran low, leaving only eight days in reserve. Doubtless Claudius also had in mind the time in 40-39 BC during the civil war when Octavian, the future Augustus, was nearly killed when starving rioters in Rome stoned him (Appian v.68).

One solution was to persuade the corn transports to continue their deliveries in winter. Claudius did this by promising that the state would underwrite any losses from winter storms, and offered subsidies to merchant shippers who continued to bring in corn (Suetonius, *Claudius* 18.2). However, building a new harbour was a much more far-reaching and permanent solution. Claudius was responsible for creating the first proper harbour facilities known as Portus, which were begun in AD 42 a couple of miles to the north of Ostia and connected to Rome by road. According to Suetonius, this was achieved by 'building up curved breakwaters on the left and right and in front of the entrance a mole in deep water' (*Claudius* 20.3). To reinforce the mole, a ship that had been used by Caligula to bring an obelisk from Egypt was sunk and secured by piles. On top of the mole Suetonius records that a lighthouse was built to guide the ships in (Fig. 1.1).

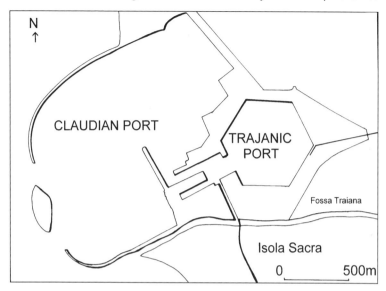

1.1. The Claudian and Trajanic harbours at Ostia.

The inspiration for the mole almost certainly came from the occasion when Claudius was visiting the construction works. A whale had been attracted by a sunken ship from Gaul carrying hides. While feeding on the cargo, the whale inadvertently dug itself into the seabed and became trapped under a mound of sand that built up over it from the waves (Pliny the Elder, *Natural History* ix.14-15; see Selected Texts).

The work took till 64 to complete, and was celebrated by Nero, Claudius' successor, who issued coins depicting the harbour and bearing the legend *Portus Augusti* (despite a disastrous storm in 62 – see below) (Fig. 1.2). In 47 Claudius had also initiated drainage works from the Tiber in the Ostia area, designed to discharge flood water into the sea rather than allow it to swamp Rome. It was a mark of Ostia's growing importance that Claudius also had to relocate a Rome urban cohort to Ostia where it could act as a fire service for the grain warehouses. Whether or not the plan was to replace the much more distant port at Puteoli as a source of food for Rome, where Egyptian grain was landed, is unknown. Either way, Puteoli continued to be extremely important.

Within little more than 50 years it proved necessary to improve the harbour works. Trajan (98-117) created a brand-new hexagonal harbour immediately east of Claudius' harbour and connected to it by channels, as part of a more general programme to improve Italy's west coast ports

1.2. Brass *sestertius* of Nero (AD 54-68), struck in 64 to commemorate the completion of the Claudian harbour at Ostia.

(Fig. 1.1). A devastating storm in AD 62 wrecked 200 ships in the Claudian harbour, at that time still not complete, but it showed that the harbour was simply too big (Tacitus, *Annals* xv.18). This, and increasing traffic, made a more secure harbour essential. However, it is extremely unlikely that the Claudian port became no more than a protective entranceway to the new facilities. It is more probable that the new Trajanic port operated in addition to the old one, vastly increasing Ostia's capacity. Each side of the new hexagonal harbour was 358 metres long. Allowing for the waterway entrance on the western side, the new harbour provided about two kilometres of docks, lined with warehouses and monuments.

A new canal, the *Fossa Traiana*, connected the port to the Tiber. Ostia became the commercial headquarters for administering the food-supply to Rome. Huge granaries were built and merchant shippers, traders in commodities, and other commercial services were based here.

By the mid-second century AD Ostia was reaching its climax, supplanting Puteoli. Intensive building activity lasted well into the third century. Temples to the Persian god Mithras, so favoured by soldiers and merchants, were built alongside bath-houses, the forum, the capitol, private houses and tenement blocks, while the tombs and gravestones of her population that lined the road to Rome and the road that ran across the Isola Sacra to the port testify to an exotic and cosmopolitan population. This was a world of the wealthy Roman elite, merchants, artisans, shopkeepers, port workers, slaves and foreigners from across the Empire.

The new port facilities inevitably attracted settlement and Ostia gradually lost importance as Portus evolved into an independent town. In the fourth century power and influence passed to Portus when Constantine I

(AD 307-337) transferred Ostia's civic rights there. Ostia continued to exist throughout the fourth century, maintaining and repairing public buildings while its private citizens continued to build elaborate town-houses. But as Rome waned in the fifth century so Ostia inevitably followed, and by the mid-sixth century the city was in terminal decay. The silting up of the Tiber and the gradual progression of the coastline further west turned the area into landlocked malarial swamps. Local settlement moved to a village fortified by Pope Gregory in the mid-ninth century, called Gregoriopolis. Ostia's ruins were left largely untouched and al-though upper storeys tended to collapse, the accumulation of debris, vegetation and silt left many of the buildings covered up to a considerable height. Indeed, some of the structures survive higher than buildings at Pompeii which were pulverized by volcanic debris (it is not always appreciated how many buildings at Pompeii are heavily restored above a height of three to four metres). However, a number of Ostian buildings have also been heavily restored in modern times, which is not always apparent without close examination.

Pompeii

Pompeii and Herculaneum were mainly centres of local commerce, local landowning interests, local politics and local concerns. Commercial, social, and political interests beyond their regions existed, but were not dominant factors. Their principal relevance to the history and archaeology of the Roman world are the freak circumstances of their destruction and preservation.

Traces of human activity in and around Pompeii dating back to before 1500 BC and continuing right down to the Iron Age in the early first millennium BC are scarcely surprising. This intensely fertile area on the volcanic soils around Vesuvius in Campania was bound to draw people. But Pompeii has naturally attracted more archaeological attention than most of the surrounding area and these traces may simply be evidence for general human use of the whole Bay of Naples area. There is increasing evidence for prehistoric settlement across the region, for example at Nuceria. Nevertheless, Pompeii is a place which is not easily available for deep stratigraphic archaeology: in some buildings the destruction this would cause is simply unacceptable. Increasingly, however, advantage is being taken of locations where targeted excavation can take place without damaging surviving buildings and floors (Fig. 1.3).

Pompeii itself lay close to the mouth of the River Sarno, making it of local strategic importance. Greek control of the region was centred on Cumae to the north-west. The most significant remains of Pompeii for this

1.3. Pompeii from the air. In the foreground are the Gladiators' Barracks and behind them the Theatre and the Odeon. At the upper left are the Stabian Baths.

phase are the Temple of Apollo and the so-called sixth-century BC Greek Doric temple in the Triangular Forum. There are several different theories for the origin of the city's name, none of them conclusive. However, it is worth noting that the name Pompeii is most closely paralleled by the Greek πομπέια ('leading in procession'), a word also used in Latin. In antiquity it was claimed that Pompeii was named after the procession led by Hercules en route from Spain into Campania. Excavations in and around the Triangular Forum have revealed sporadic traces of wooden and other simple buildings ranging in date from as far back as at least the seventh century BC to the second century BC.

This Triangular Forum lies beside the area where the street grid shows distinct differences from the rest of the enlarged town of Roman date and sits on a volcanic outcrop from a primeval eruption. It has long been suggested that this zone represents the original Pompeii, the 'old city', around which the later city developed, and this certainly seems the most likely interpretation. But traces of more contemporary settlement have been found across Pompeii, reflecting its later lay-out, and it has been suggested that much of the area we now recognize as Pompeii had in reality been occupied at more or less the same time even if it was originally little more than a fortified community of farms with a town-like nucleus.

Power struggles in Italy led to a phase when the Etruscans seem to have dominated the area, only to be followed by the Oscan-speaking Samnites who seized the town of Capua, some 40 kilometres north-west of Pompeii in 423 BC. By the fourth century BC Pompeii was just one of a number of settlements under Samnite control, and occupation seems to have become denser. Limited archaeological exploration below some of Pompeii's later Roman-date houses has revealed traces of earlier buildings of this period. By 290 BC, when the Samnite Wars ended, Pompeii was an insignificant country town. As one of Rome's allies, Pompeii had to supply troops for Rome's wars, but Pompeians nonetheless retained control over their own local affairs and their own identity.

Pompeii experienced a period of rapid growth during the third and second centuries BC. It had a theatre by at least the second century BC and possibly earlier (Fig. 1.3). New roads were laid out as part of a town plan which seemed to take account of existing occupation while laying out regimented plots known as *insulae* within the walled area. Pompeian magistrates recorded on inscriptions the laying out of the new roads and were clearly administering the city in a way that was very similar to Roman customs. To begin with these land divisions may have been allocated as farmland to accommodate an increasing population. The reason for the growth is unknown but is likely to have been linked to the disorder of the Second Punic War (218-202 BC) during which the Carthaginian general Hannibal invaded Italy. Certainly the city was well-protected, with seven fortified gates. In the second century BC, as the city's wealth grew, these plots were increasingly built up with town-houses, and by the first century BC many of Pompeii's well-known atrium-courtyard houses were extant. The same families who could afford these new homes were also busy contributing to Pompeii's public build-ings and facilities as expressions of their influence, munificence and wealth. The forum and some of its associated buildings, such as the Temple of Jupiter, belong to this phase. Nevertheless, some of the old traditions endured. Oscan, the language of the Samnites, was used for some inscriptions including early political slogans, showing that it prob-ably remained an everyday language for most of the population at least for the moment.

The only major disruption to this process was the Social War of 91-89 BC when Rome's Italian allies revolted. Pompeii and Herculaneum re-mained loyal to rebellious forces dominated by the Samnite peoples of southern Italy and paid the price. The Roman general Lucius Cornelius Sulla destroyed the nearby town of Stabiae. Traces of artillery damage to Pompeii's solid walls bear witness to Sulla's assault on the city in 89 BC.

Other traces of damage have been found within the city. Pompeii and Herculaneum fell to Sulla. In 80 BC Pompeii was made into a Roman colony by Publius Cornelius Sulla, the general Sulla's nephew. He installed loyal Roman citizens to ensure Pompeii remained reliable and loyal to its Roman masters. Now renamed *Colonia Cornelia Veneria Pompeianorum* ('The Cornelian Venerian Colony of Pompeians') after Lucius Cornelius Sulla and his assumed patron Venus, the transition to this new status meant land being requisitioned for allocation to Sulla's military veterans and their families.

As a Roman colony, Pompeii was supposed to set a shining example of Roman peace and civic order as well as acting as a trained military reserve in case of further rebellions. Old Samnite traditions retreated into Pompeii's past. The presence of Roman military veterans, their tastes, and more especially their skills, played a large part in the evolution of Pompeii into a full-scale Roman city. Public buildings were added or elaborated, including the earliest known permanent amphitheatre, which was built in the extreme south-east of the city.

It is hard to see why the Pompeians would have accepted control of their town passing to imported Roman colonists, since it was bound to have been at their expense, and it seems that they did not. In 63 BC a senatorial rebel called Lucius Sergius Catilina tried to take over the Roman state in a violent insurrection. He was roundly defeated but Publius Cornelius Sulla was accused of using violence to help him, and also of causing friction between the Pompeian colonists and the ordinary townspeople. The Roman lawyer and politician Cicero defended Sulla in court. Cicero claimed that the tension in Pompeii had been there for many years, and that Sulla had worked tirelessly on behalf of both colonists and the original inhabitants. However, Cicero conceded that making Pompeii a colony had not been entirely in the interests of the Pompeians though it is unlikely it ever was only supposed to be for their exclusive benefit. Cicero said, 'the fortune of the Roman state has separated the interests of the colonists from the fortunes of the native Pompeians' (*pro Sulla* 62). If the evidence of inscriptions at Pompeii is correct, it appears that the Pompeians generally found themselves abruptly excluded from holding civic office in the years immediately after 80 BC, an abuse which needed correcting.

Pompeii under the emperors
For much of the remaining first century BC the Roman world was convulsed by civil wars. Pompeii seems to have been generally unaffected by these dramatic events. Wealthy Romans bought property in the vicinity,

1.4. Pompeii: House of the Menander, the main visual axis through the *atrium*, across the *tablinum* to the *peristylium*. Skilful adjustment of column spacing in the *peristylium* maximized the effect of the axis which also disguised the asymmetrical layout of the house.

including Cicero who owned a farm near Pompeii, a place he used as a bolt-hole from Rome. Once the civil wars were over by the late first century BC and Augustus had established himself as the first emperor (27 BC-AD 14), Pompeii's wealth grew apace. The town's premier citizens vied with one another to endow Pompeii with public monuments honouring Augustus, his family, his principles and his rule. The city was equipped with all the necessary public buildings to fulfil the formal religious, administrative and leisure requirements of a Roman urban settlement: temples, forum, basilica, market buildings (including the remarkable Building of Eumachia), theatre, amphitheatre, baths and gymnasia. The houses of the Pompeian elite mirrored these expressions of civic status (Fig. 1.4).

Only on odd occasions did Pompeii make headlines. In AD 59 a riot took place in the town amphitheatre. Citizens of Nuceria, a nearby town, arrived to support their favourite gladiators in a show put on by a disgraced senator called Livineius Regulus and soon became engaged in a slanging match with the Pompeians. The words turned to stones and then swords were drawn. Unfortunately for the Nucerians there were many more Pompeian supporters and the result was a number of dead and injured visitors, including children. News reached an outraged Senate in Rome and further gladiatorial displays there were banned for a decade. Livineius and his associates, presumably including the presiding Pompeian magistrates, were forced into exile (Tacitus, *Annals* xiv.17).

In 62 or early 63 a disastrous earthquake demolished, according to Tacitus, *magna ex parte* ('the greater part') of Pompeii (*Annals* xv.22). Tacitus placed it in what we would call 62, Seneca placed it in 63. It makes no practical difference. It is not possible now to be certain which is correct, though in this book 62 will be used. Other earthquakes and tremors probably followed. This pre-eruption seismic activity was more responsible for Pompeii's present ruinous state than many visitors appreciate. Even more damage was caused by post-eruption scavengers in antiquity and the effects of early excavation work which exposed buildings without properly consolidating them. This would help explain the extensive evidence for ongoing repair work in public and private buildings found across the city. In 79 the forum resembled a building site, though even this may be partly due to the recovery of marble in ancient and medieval times. A number of private houses were still being repaired in 79, and the opportunity was being taken in some cases to make extravagant improvements, including ostentatious wall-paintings (Fig. 1.5).

The water-supply system which distributed water to public baths, public fountains and private houses was severely disrupted by the earthquake of 62 or later tremors and was still being patched up in 79. Many private houses had had to make do without water supplies, leaving their garden fountains and features redundant. The general disruption may have increased the opportunism of the Pompeians who had for some time been taking an increasingly lax attitude to the public lands around the city's walls, helping themselves to plots for building. Inscriptions record how an imperial tribune, Titus Suedius Clemens, was sent by the emperor Vespasian (69-79) to clear out these encroachments not only at Pompeii but also elsewhere in Italy, suggesting that this was a widespread problem (CC F109). In the city's last decades there seems to have been a considerable increase in the provision of self-contained apartments in and around the existing large houses. This may have begun as early as Augustan times, though the earthquake of 62 may well have speeded the process up.

Herculaneum

Little is known of Herculaneum's history. It was said to have been founded by Hercules, which suggests that it was a Greek city first, reflected in the Greek-like proportions of its street grid, though it may have had an Etruscan phase. The rest of its history is likely to have mirrored Pompeii's, becoming a Samnite settlement before being ab-

1.5. Pompeii. House of the Vettii. On a painting just inside the entrance of a house owned by wealthy freedmen brothers, Priapus weighs his manhood against a moneybag in an image that could have come from the pages of Petronius' *Satyricon*. Painted in the last few years of the city's life.

sorbed under Roman control. So much less of the city has been uncovered that we know little about its evolution, though it may also have been made into a Roman colony in 80 BC by Sulla after the Social War.

By the mid-first century AD Herculaneum had become an elegant coastal resort characterized by well-appointed townhouses overlooking the Bay of Naples and surrounded by the country villas of wealthy Romans for whom the region provided an elegant retreat (Fig. 1.6). However, since only around a quarter of the town has been excavated, it may not be representative of the whole of the original settlement.

Herculaneum's location between two streams probably prevented the town from growing to anything like Pompeii's size. Unfortunately it will never be possible to excavate the whole site to find out. Like Pompeii, Herculaneum undoubtedly suffered from the earthquake of 62; an inscription of Vespasian records the restoration of the Temple of the Mother

1.6. A Herculaneum street. In the centre is the House in Opus Craticium and to the right, part of the House of the Wooden Partition. A bench for waiting clients can be seen at the lower right (see p. 25).

Goddess. Its houses also show signs of marked changes of usage in the city's latter decades with an increasing emphasis on cramming more accommodation into smaller areas as the population grew and land became more expensive. This is most obvious today in buildings such as the House in Opus Craticium (Fig. 1.6, and see pp. 78-9), and the Samnite House (see pp. 68-70).

Chapter 2

Government and Social Structure

The origins of Roman society

Early Roman society was made up largely of free citizens (*plebs*) but they were dominated by a small group of aristocratic families (*patricii*) whose elite status was defined by their wealth in land. The patricians controlled all aspects of Roman society and were determined to maintain that control. The system began to break down by the mid-fifth century BC when the ban on intermarriage between patricians and plebeians was lifted so that patrician families could absorb the wealth acquired by some of the more successful plebeians.

By the third century BC the wealthy plebeians and the old patricians were more or less indistinguishable. These were the nobles (*nobiles*), members of the families who could fulfil the property qualification (one million sesterces by imperial times) for their men to pursue a career as a senator and magistrate. The rest of the free citizen population of Rome in theory voted for these magistracies but in practice the nobles manipulated the entire system through their patronage, influence and financial muscle.

Rome's 'town council' was the Senate, mainly drawn from the ranks of those who had entered a senatorial career by being elected one of the twenty *quaestores* magistrates at about 25 years of age. A successful career (*cursus honorum*) in subsequent magistracies climaxed in being elected one of the two consuls which led to proconsular status and eligibility for (among other jobs) the most important provincial governorships. None of these posts was ever held by fewer than two men, to prevent any one individual taking supreme power. Under the emperors this system persisted, but in practice it was the emperor who recruited senators and influenced appointments to the senatorial magistracies, often holding one of the consulships himself. He held the power of tribune of the plebs, which allowed him legitimately to veto senatorial legislation.

The senatorial elite usually had little direct impact on towns like Pompeii because they had bigger fish to fry in Rome and in the government of provinces. But Ostia, so vital as the port of entry for Rome, in early imperial times had its own *quaestor* (a relatively junior senatorial magistracy) in charge of administering any grain shipments arriving there.

As the post was so important, the Ostian *quaestor* seems to have had the status of a man who had served in the more senior magistracy of a *praetor*. As the Roman Empire grew, wealthy and important provincials were drawn into the Senate by far-sighted emperors such as Claudius (AD 41-54) who saw that Rome's future depended on giving such people a stake in the system. Such men played the same role in their provincial cities as the traditional senators had played in Rome. Marcus Nonius Balbus, tribune of the plebs in 32 BC, and later proconsular governor of Crete and Cyrenaica, dominated the civic scene in Herculaneum in the late first century BC. A number of monuments testify to the gifts he bestowed on the city, which included rebuilding the basilica, and the honours Herculaneum awarded him (Fig. 2.1; see also Selected Texts).

In theory senators avoided commerce and trade which were seen as 'beneath' the dignity of their status. In reality they were often closely involved, operating through their freedmen and slaves (see for example Marcus Crassus Frugi, p. 53). But below the senatorial class came the equestrians (*equites*). The name came from Rome's early days when it referred to those men who could afford to furnish a horse for their military service. By the late third century BC equestrians had become involved in

2.1. The terrace outside the Suburban Baths with the tomb of Marcus Nonius Balbus, patron of Herculaneum, commemorating his gifts to the city and the honours paid him. The statue is a replica of the original.

commerce, now of increasing importance. Under Tiberius in AD 22 equestrians became recognized as a class (*ordo*) in their own right. The property qualification was 400,000 sesterces. Equestrians were used as a source of administrators across the Empire, commanders of auxiliary military units, and as a handy source of new senators. Once the Claudian port was operational at Ostia, the senatorial *quaestor* was replaced with equestrian procurators who reported to the equestrian Prefect of the Grain Supply (*Praefectus Annonae*) at Rome. Very few Pompeians reached even the status of equestrians, Marcus Holconius Rufus being an exception (see below, p. 25).

Roman citizens, Latins and provincials

The remainder of Roman society was made up of ordinary free citizens, Latin citizens, provincials, freedmen and slaves. The Roman citizen enjoyed certain rights, such as the right to vote and immunity from summary imprisonment. Slaves had very few rights, but could be freed. Vast numbers of people were freed slaves or the descendants of freed slaves. Freedmen and their families played an increasingly important role in civic life, especially in the commercial enterprises operated at Ostia and Pompeii.

Roman citizenship was held by the children of citizens and those awarded citizenship, for example as a result of military service, those who petitioned for it from the emperor, and those who were freed from slavery by their citizen owners. Roman citizenship was traditionally advertised through possession of the three-part name, the *tria nomina*. This consisted of a *praenomen*, *nomen*, and *cognomen*. The *praenomen* was a personal name, the *nomen* the clan to which one belonged, and the *cognomen* either the branch of the clan or simply a personal name. Thus Gaius Julius Caesar is Gaius, member of the Caesar branch of the Julian clan. Freed slaves acquired the first two parts of their name from their old masters, with the *cognomen* being their old personal slave name or sometimes alluding to their status (see below). Roman citizens belonged to one of the 35 voting tribes, which entitled them to vote in elections in Rome. This number never increased, and as the population of citizens grew across the Empire the voting privilege became increasingly irrelevant since the vast majority were too far from Rome ever to exercise the right. In AD 212 the declaration of universal citizenship by Caracalla (211-217) made all free men within the Empire's borders into Roman citizens.

Latin citizenship was devised as an intermediate status for Roman allies in Italy in the third century BC. Latins enjoyed some of the privileges of Roman citizenship. In 89 BC at the end of the Social War the Italian

Latins, and this included citizens of places like Pompeii and Herculaneum, became Roman citizens. Latin citizenship continued to be awarded to other provincials as a stepping stone to full citizenship. Free provincials were known as *peregrini*. They enjoyed the rights of their own community, but had to give these up if they became Roman citizens. As *peregrini* they had no rights or political status in Roman communities.

An advertisement for rental property in the estate of Julia Felix at Pompeii gives an idea about how persons of high social class in a provincial town liked to be regarded, and how their custom was sought. The advertisement announces that among the properties available are baths suitable only for the *nongenti* to rent. The *nongenti* were a class of 900 equestrians who supervised the elections at Rome. It cannot possibly be referring to them. Pompeii may have had its own local equivalent of the *nongenti* but it is more likely that the advertisement is suggesting the baths are of a standard suitable only for people of such high status. The seventeenth-century English diarist John Evelyn (1620-1706) announced in the preamble to his book *Sylva* that it was designed only for 'persons of quality', and not those of the 'meaner capacities'. Likewise, the Julia Felix estate administrators were appealing to Pompeii's 'persons of quality', or those with social pretensions, to make sure no riff-raff tried to lease the property (CC H44, but note that *nongenti* is translated there merely as 'respectable people').

The *familia*

The core component of Roman society at every level was the family (*familia*), which included the extended family and its freedmen and slaves, overseen by the senior male, the *pater familias* ('master of the household'), even if members were living in different houses. He had total power over his *familia*, making all the decisions affecting any of them, including marriage and punishments. He controlled all their property and represented their political interests. He also acted as family priest. This power was called *patria potestas*. Most importantly of all, the *pater familias* was the only member of the family who was recognized as an individual in law.

Patron and client

Roman society was built around a hierarchy of interdependence between ranks. Patrons, men of higher status, needed their clients (*clientes*; the origin of the word 'client' is the word *cluere*, 'to hear oneself called'). These men were lesser business associates, and sometimes also freedmen of the patron (see the section on freedmen below, pp. 32-4). A man's clients were often members of the same trade association (see the section on *collegia* below, pp. 37-8). In return for their patron's protection and the honour of being associated with him, they voted for him and supported him financially when he was in public office. They might also work for him, offer him advantageous deals, and return him favours when he looked after their financial problems or family affairs. Having plenty of clients was a sign of status, and especially useful to the politically ambitious. Outside the House of the Wooden Partition in Herculaneum are the remains of benches where clients waited to appeal to their patron, show their support, or simply pay their respects (see Fig. 1.6), a feature paralleled outside numerous other houses in Pompeii.

Civic government: *aediles* and *duoviri*

All cities in the Roman Empire were governed by a system that emulated Rome's Republican administration of senators and magistrates. Like Rome, provincial urban government was exclusively a male affair – women had no political status though they expected to influence political events and elections. For a Pompeian man, achieving office in civic government was the crowning glory of his political and social career, but he had to be freeborn and have the necessary wealth and resources. As a young man he set out on this route by competing for election as one of the junior pair of civic magistrates, the *aediles*, not to be confused with the senatorial magistracy in Rome of the same name. Elected annually in March, and taking up office on 1 July, the civic *aediles* had responsibilities for the town's public and religious buildings, roads, sewers, aqueducts and so on (Figs 2.2 and 2.4).

An ex-*aedile* in theory automatically became a town councillor (*decurion*) and could then stand for election after around three years as one of the two annual *duoviri* ('the two men'; singular *duumvir*). Since only an ex-*aedile* could stand to be a *duumvir*, the most competitive electioneering at Pompeii concerned the entry position of *aedile*. Promotion to the duumvirate was effectively automatic. The reason for pairing these magistracies, as in Rome, was to prevent one individual becoming too powerful. Nevertheless, it was possible for an individual occasionally to be re-elected as a *duumvir*. Thus Numerius Herennius Celsus served as *duumvir* twice at Pompeii in the early first century AD, though some men were re-elected three, four or more times (CC G5). Marcus Holconius Rufus was *duumvir* five times and served twice as a *quinquennalis* between the late first century BC and early first century AD (CC D53-4).

2.2. Pompeii: Tomb of Gaius Vestorius Priscus outside the Vesuvian Gate.
Priscus was *aedile* when he died at the age of 22. He was honoured with 2,000
sesterces to pay for his funeral and the place for his tomb, which his mother
paid for. Probably AD 76 (CC F88).

Civic government: property qualifications and obligations of office

Every five years the civic *duoviri* were elected as *quinquennales* and had
special powers to carry out a census. The successful candidates had
usually already served as ordinary *duoviri* in previous years. The *quinquennales* compiled a census of those eligible to serve as magistrates and
serve on the council by possessing the correct property qualification. In
an important city in Italy this could be as much as 100,000 sesterces. In a
small North African city it was around 20,000 sesterces. At Pompeii,
Herculaneum or Ostia somewhere between 50-100,000 sesterces is probably about right. Presumably the census afforded opportunities to manipu-
late assessments to ensure desirables were recruited, and undesirables
excluded. The census was not just an elitist conceit. Being a magistrate
brought substantial financial obligations to the community and it was
essential a candidate could pay his way (see Public Munificence, below).

It is easy to see how the Pompeian municipal aristocracy could remain
in the hands of a relatively small circle of wealthy families (Fig. 2.3).
Writing in the fifth century AD, more than 300 years after Pompeii was
destroyed and 450 years since the date of his (now lost) source, Macrobius
recorded that Cicero mocked how Caesar ignored the usual election

2.3. Pompeii. Statue base commemorating Marcus Lucretius Decidianus, who served as *duumvir* three times, *quinquennalis*, priest, military tribune by popular acclaim, and military engineering officer. Set up by decree of the councillors after his death. Late first century BC or early first century AD (CC F92).

process when finding places for his friends in the Senate. When Cicero was asked by Publius Mallius to expedite his stepson's entry to the town council (*Saturnalia* ii.3.11), Cicero replied with *Romae si vis habebit; Pompeis est difficile*, 'at Rome, if you want, he shall have it; at Pompeii it is troublesome'. This is normally used as evidence that it was far harder to get into Pompeii's council because it was run by a self-serving elite than it was to enter the Senate in Rome. However, Cicero's real concern was to express his sarcastic disdain for Caesar's corrupt practices. If anything, Pompeii is being described as a town where a place on the council at least required the rigour of an election process. But this should not disguise the fact that the evidence from Pompeii itself and also Herculaneum and Ostia is of certain families who tended to dominate local politics for generations. Cicero was not idealizing Pompeii; it was just that Rome was even worse.

Marcus Holconius Rufus went on to become 'patron of the colony', which meant that he represented Pompeii's interests in Rome. He had also been made a 'military tribune by popular (demand)'. This was not the genuine military command (awarded by the emperor), but a purely honorific title awarded by the local council. Exceptionally for a Pompeïan, Rufus reached equestrian status, placing him in the Roman world's second highest social rank. A statue of him, probably posthumous and almost certainly adapted from one that originally represented a member of the imperial family, was erected in the centre of Pompeii and thus conveniently suggested that he was of even more exalted status.

A curious aside concerns the emperor Gaius ('Caligula', AD 37-41), who became notorious for the lunatic and murderous activities of the latter part of his reign. After his death, many inscriptions naming him were erased and statues of him toppled. But the Pompeians had originally nursed considerable respect for Caligula: they made him an honorary *duumvir* when he was still only heir (in 34) and again in the last year of his reign (40-41). Obviously, Caligula took no part in Pompeii's government and instead a prefect was appointed to carry out the duties. But the gesture provided reflected glory for those Pompeians who filled the post in other years, before or after. Ironically Holconius Rufus' statue had very probably originally been one of Caligula.

Civic government: the council and councillors
The town council (*ordo decurionum* or sometimes *curia*) was a body normally of around 100 councillors (*decuriones*), each of whom had in theory served as an *aedile* and been assessed as fulfilling the local property qualification. Would-be councillors were also supposed to be at least 25 years old, though this could be waived, and held the position for life. Not every freeborn citizen was eligible, even if he had the property qualification. Gravediggers, gladiators, shopkeepers, comedy actors, and owners of small businesses were excluded, another component in a system that helped restrict membership to a local elite.

A curious phenomenon at Pompeii was the occasional nomination of children to the town council. Two boys of the wealthy Lucretii Valentes family were promoted this way, one (aged eight) explicitly as a reward for providing gladiatorial fights along with his father. Both boys died young and their privileged positions are recorded on their tombstones, which is the only reason we know about them (CC G21, 24). Another was Marcus Alleius Libella, who had already become a councillor by the time he died at the age of 17 (CC F87). It may have been a convenient device to make sure the council was made up of the 'right people' by influential and wealthy families rewarding themselves this way and thus perpetuating their grip on local politics. Unfortunately we have no idea how common this was or to what extent adult councillors had held their positions since childhood (but see Publius Celerius Amandus under *Collegia* below). It was also a route by which generous freedmen could be rewarded through their freeborn sons (see Numerius Popidius Celsinus below). Another possibility is that incorporating under-age boys from appropriate families helped make up the decurions to the correct total when there was a shortage of men who fulfilled the property qualification.

The council had ultimate charge of the town budget, state religion, public buildings and land. The *duoviri* supervised the council's meetings. As a body the council issued decrees (*decreta*) such as an instruction to repair a public building or road. These were referred to on inscriptions as *decreto decurionum* ('by decree of the councillors'), usually abbreviated to DD, and were carried out by the *aediles* or *duoviri*, depending on the task (Fig. 2.3). Describing it thus makes the system sound very formal. In practice it was probably much more ad hoc, with factions cutting deals at the games or at the baths. Pompeii's small-town politics was bound to involve intimidation, corruption, and indifference, as well as genuinely motivated good men.

The council was self-regulating and autonomous but when events got out of control, the Senate in Rome could take over and impose draconian sanctions to re-establish order. At Pompeii this took place in AD 59 after the murderous riot in the amphitheatre (see p. 17). This occasion was alarming enough not only for the current *duoviri*, Gnaeus Pompeius Grosphus and Grosphus Pompeius Gavianus, to be replaced with new men for the rest of their term, but also for a prefect, Sextus Pompeius Proculus, to be installed at Pompeii in what must have been some sort of supervisory capacity to make sure there was no repetition of the disgraceful event (CC D35-6).

Electioneering and campaign slogans
No other Roman town has produced as much evidence for electioneering as Pompeii. Free citizens were eligible to vote and this was organized by dividing a town into voting districts, in Pompeii's case five. Within the districts support for candidates came from individuals (often associates of the candidate) or special interest groups. Walls across the city were routinely daubed with the name of a candidate and his qualities by his supporters. These slogans, *programmata*, were painted over and replaced with new ones in succeeding years. Lucius Ceius Secundus stood for *duumvir* in the town's latter days. Secundus lived close to the centre of Pompeii. A number of electoral slogans remain visibly daubed on the

2.4. Pompeii, Via dell'Abbondanza: electoral slogan promoting the election of a *duumvir* (II.VIR) and an *aedile* (AED).

walls of his house. He served as *aedile, duumvir* twice, and *quinquennalis*. His campaign in early AD 79 to become *duumvir* involved running alongside Gnaeus Helvius Sabinus who was standing for *aedile*, a man who ran an especially conspicuous campaign for this crucial opportunity to enter a career in civic office (CC F35ff., especially F67). Being associated with Secundus was evidently seen as an advantage. In Pompeii Epidius Sabinus would have taken it for granted that his client Trebius would publicly support him by having a political slogan painted on a wall asking that any passing voter help elect Sabinus a *duumvir* (CC F112).

Occasionally the slogans point out the benefits a candidate might bring to Pompeii. Gaius Julius Polybius, standing for election as an *aedile*, was said to be a source of good bread while Tiberius Claudius Verus, standing for *duumvir*, was simply said to be honest (CC F8, F5). These slogans were frequently abbreviated. O.V.F. appears on many of them, representing *oro vos faciatis*, 'I beg that you make [name of the candidate] *aedile*' or '*duumvir*', as appropriate. Another abbreviated slogan was D.D.R.P., short for *dicendo dignum rei publicae*, 'celebrated as worthy of public office' (Fig. 2.4). The cut and thrust of electioneering also involved knocking the opposition. Marcus Cerrinius Vatia's enemies painted up slogans saying that those fast asleep, thieves, and drinkers, would be voting for him (CC F13).

Public munificence
Endowing towns with public monuments, facilities or services was an integral part, or even the price, of high social status or aspirations to it. It was, in essence, the social rent – a mixture of honourable *noblesse oblige*, expectation and habit, and the naked buying of popularity. Such philan-

thropy was the gateway to power. Men bought status and popularity for themselves by fulfilling a legal obligation to provide buildings or games for the public good during their term in a magistracy. It was also a gesture with which these men acknowledged their individual debt to the emperor as the father of a social system that had provided them with the opportunity to hold office and echoed the work of the emperors, not only in Rome but also in cities throughout the Empire.

At the top of the scale were Roman senators who might live locally or have family origins in a provincial town. Among other gifts, Pliny the Younger had wanted to provide 500,000 sesterces to be used to educate poor freeborn Italian children in his home town of *Comum* (Como). Anxious that the capital sum would simply be squandered by the town (an interesting comment on how funds might be misused by civic authorities), he instead handed over land of that value to an agent in *Comum* and then rented it back. This way he paid an annual rent of 30,000 sesterces (or 6%) back to *Comum* to use his own land. The technique preserved the capital sum, and would survive his death since the rent was far less than the market value of the land (*Letters* vii.18). The gift of the capital sum was recorded on an inscription installed on *Comum*'s public baths, along with his gift of the baths.

In provincial towns, the local elite behaved in much the same way, but on a more modest scale. A late first-century BC inscription from *Iguvium* (Gubbo) in Italy records a magistrate called Gnaeus Satrius Rufus who had spent 7,750 sesterces of his own money on games, 6,200 to restore a temple of Diana, 3450 to provide supplies for the legions, and a further 6,000 sesterces just for the 'dignity' of his status (*ILS* 5531).

In Pompeii Marcus Holconius Rufus and Marcus Holconius Celer paid for facilities in the theatre including boxes and seating (CC D51). Other inscriptions from the building specify the choice made by certain magistrates to provide seating or other facilities *rather* than laying on games. Marcus Tullius, who served as *duumvir* three times, supplied a plot of his own land near Pompeii's forum for a temple of Augustan Fortune and paid for the building (CC E32). Many other examples are cited in Chapter 3.

The *magistri* of the Fortunate Augustan Suburban Country District at Pompeii seem to have been equally entitled to pay for seating in the amphitheatre or to put on games. An inscription from Pompeii's amphitheatre records that *pro ludis* ('in place of games'), seats had been installed by the *magistri*, fulfilling a decree by Pompeii's town council that they do so (CC D1). The social status of the suburban *magistri* was thus quite distinct from the decurial class but it showed parallels, and they were accorded the respect of a council decree as were the civic magistrates.

Likewise, freedmen could contribute to a town. They could not buy their own way into office, but they could buy it for their freeborn sons.

Freedmen and social status

If a freedman was freed by a Roman citizen, and official procedure followed, then the freedman became a Roman citizen too. He adopted his master's *praenomen* and *nomen* and added his former slave name as a *cognomen*. Thus we have the freedman Marcus Petacius Dasius at Pompeii, whose freeborn son Marcus Petacius Severus was a member of the Menenian voting tribe (CC G32). It was also possible for a slave to be freed through less formal routes such as private declaration, but this could lead to legal disputes about when this had occurred, with implications for the freedman or freedwoman's children.

An excellent way to amass loyal clients was for a patron to free his most reliable slaves. In return for their freedom they supported their former master's interests. Such men often followed their patron's business, having been trained in it. At Ostia the corn merchant Publius Aufidius Fortis took a prominent role in town government and the corn merchants' guild in the mid-second century AD. Men holding office in the guild and bearing the name Publius Aufidius in later years were probably his freedmen. For a man like Aufidius Fortis, surrounding himself with advocates whose loyalty to his family could last after his death was clearly attractive. The architect of major modifications made to Pompeii's theatre in Augustus's time was a freedman, Marcus Artorius Primus, recorded on an inscription displayed on the building (CC D52). He probably trained while enslaved, and was rewarded for his skills by being freed. It is highly unusual for an architect to be commemorated by name; the text may have had the added benefit of publicizing the Artorii family that had freed him.

Freedmen and freedwomen made up a large proportion of the Roman population and this was especially true of the population of successful commercial towns like Ostia and Pompeii. Excluded from political office by their status, they nevertheless played a vitally important commercial role in city life. Freedmen formed a substantial part of the membership of trade associations (see *Collegia* below). However, their freeborn children were not excluded from political office, so a freedman knew that his success could play a decisive role in the fate of his descendants. In cities like Ostia and Pompeii it is clear that the sons and grandsons of successful freedmen could compete for civic magistracies and sit on the council.

Freedmen were eligible for membership of the priesthood of one branch of the imperial cult (the *seviri Augustales*), with a board of such priests in each town (Fig. 2.5). It was one of the few routes to high status

2.5. Herculaneum. Inscriptions confirm this building, close to the basilica, to have been the headquarters of the *Augustales* priests of the imperial cult. The shrine area contains Fourth Style paintings depicting Hercules.

open to freedmen, and was an office in which they could serve alongside freeborn men. This afforded them access to the controlling group in a town in a position they could serve in alongside the magistrates and councillors. Like the magistrates, the *seviri Augustales* were obliged to pay for public monuments or entertainments during their time in office.

By the late first century AD at the earliest the board had been organized into a hierarchy of varying numbers. Although election was involved it also seems that cash payments played a part in buying one's way in. This limited the candidates to successful men and formalized their identity as members of the freedmen aristocracy. Although nominally a religious organization, in the Roman world formal religion was inextricably linked with social, political and financial status. The *seviri Augustales* functioned much as the commercial guilds did and naturally the most important members were prominent in their own trade guilds.

The prestige of membership of the *seviri Augustales* reflected the honours heaped on prominent freeborn councillors and magistrates. Lucius Mammius Maximus, an *Augustalis* and freedman at Herculaneum, was awarded a lifesize bronze statue of himself by the 'citizens and other residents', displayed in the theatre. At Pompeii Gaius Munatius Faustus, voted the honour of a special place for his tomb (see Chapter 5), was a freedman of considerable status. At Ostia the freedman Publius Horatius Chryseros donated the sum of 50,000 sesterces to the coffers of the priesthood. In return a statue was erected in his memory in AD 182. Part of the money had been set aside to fund the appointment of a relative as a *curator* (treasurer) to the priesthood, and other funds provided to make a modest cash donation to each of Ostia's town councillors.

Successful freedmen had close relationships with the magistrates and councillors. Appropriately targeted donations could make sure their male descendants had the social prominence and wealth to be elected as magistrates and enter the council. This was not enough for some, who found creative ways round the rules. At Pompeii Numerius Popidius Ampliatus was almost certainly a freedman, and had evidently grown wealthy and influential. His name derives from *ampliare*, 'to ennoble' or 'to amplify', which is conveniently appropriate. The city fathers of Pompeii were anxious to see him rewarded for his success and doubtless his friendship to them and the community. His freeborn six-year-old son, Numerius Popidius Celsinus, would be eligible to stand for office when he reached adulthood. Ampliatus was not willing to wait, so he provided the funds to rebuild the Temple of Isis after the earthquake of 62 in his son's name. Celsinus was promptly elected a town councillor (see Selected Inscriptions, pp. 113-14, and CC C5). This way Ampliatus was awarded with the proxy prestige and power of a status he could not legally hold, but which he could now exercise through his son.

The relationship between freedmen and Romans who could claim a freeborn ancestry was not always so mutually supportive. The celebrated *Satyricon* by Petronius mocked the vulgarity and ostentation of the fictitious freedman millionaire Trimalchio. His self-indulgence and extravagant consumption were probably devised as a way to parody the emperor Nero's lifestyle, but the joke would only have had a meaning if it was based on a popular image of wealthy freedmen as upstarts who had neither the education nor the taste to disguise their origins.

Most freedmen were modest traders, artisans and workers whose enterprise underpinned so much of the commercial side of Rome. Today, one of the best-preserved buildings at Ostia is the storehouse of the freedmen Epagathus and Epaphroditus, built in the middle of the second century AD (Fig. 2.6). Few freedmen will ever have been wealthy enough to buy their sons' way to office. But they were free to support legitimate candidates for election to magistracies, and did so on some of the electoral slogans found in Pompeii, acting in this capacity as loyal clients to their patrons. No wonder then that in the *Satyricon* Trimalchio announces, 'I am appointing one of my freedmen to be in charge of my burial place, to see that the rabble don't come running and dirtying up my monument' (*Satyricon* 71).

2.6. Ostia. The warehouse of the freedmen Epagathus and Epaphroditus, built in the middle of the second century AD. Freedmen played a vital role in urban commercial life.

Commemorating and rewarding public service

The proconsul Marcus Nonius Balbus expected to have his gifts to Herculaneum acknowledged and they duly were. A statue of the town's patron was erected in a small square on the route down from the town to the seashore. It stood beside his tomb monument, in which his cremated remains have recently been found, carved with an inscription that recorded the obligation owed by every citizen of Herculaneum to him. It added that the decurions had decided to set up an equestrian statue to Balbus in a busy place where it would be seen by many people (the surviving statue is not equestrian). They also decided that the annual *Parentalia* festival would start from his tomb, and that thereafter during the games his honorific double seat (*bisellium*) in the theatre would remain reserved for him (see Selected Inscriptions, p. 114). The grateful townsfolk had also erected a collection of statues of the whole Balbus family in the basilica that Marcus Nonius had paid to have rebuilt. The building was even known to the city as the *Basilica Noniana*, recorded in a wax tablet of AD 61, many years after its benefactor's death.

Careers in civic government were proudly recounted on tombstones of the men concerned, or of members of their families, to add to the honour of dedicated seats in the theatre and amphitheatre in their lifetimes. It was

2.7. Pompeii: Tomb of Gaius Calventius Quietus, *Augustalis* and probable freedman, *c.* AD 54-70. The tomb proudly records the honorific *bisellium* awarded for his generosity by decree of the councillors (CC G37).

not only magistrates and their families who received such honours. An *Augustalis* (and thus probably a freedman) called Gaius Calventius Quietus was awarded a *bisellium* by Pompeii's government in return for his generosity and the fact was prominently announced on his tombstone, complete with a carving of the seat (Fig. 2.7, and see Chapter 5). Other honorific testimonies to their achievements are to be found on statue bases which obliging town councils ordered in their honour (see Fig. 2.3).

Suburban administration

The *suburbanus pagus* ('suburban country district') was territory outside the town. Pompeii certainly had such a zone, called the Fortunate Augustan Suburban Country District, but today it is impossible to know exactly where this was or how far it extended. Its administrators, called *magistri* ('presidents'), had direct links to the city government. Unlike the civic magistracies, presidencies of the Suburban District at Pompeii were open to freedmen like Marcus Arrius Diomedes (CC F98). The Suburban District could pay for statues and other honours for prominent individuals, such as the herm of Norbanus Sorex displayed at Pompeii's Temple of Isis (CC D70).

Collegia

Collegia were commercial guilds open to freeborn and freedmen merchants and were a curious mix of the Masonic lodge and trade union. They provided a useful opportunity for men of substance, regardless of their status, to mingle and hold office on an equal footing. *Collegia* were notorious for their factionalism, rivalry and their increasingly dominant role in day-to-day urban politics in the last days of the Roman Republic when political leaders like Caesar and Pompey used them as hired gangs of thugs. Augustus crushed the more dangerous *collegia*, and placed strict controls on approved *collegia*, but they remained a potent force with equivalents in every Roman city where there was a thriving mercantile base.

Collegia were involved in almost all Ostia's commercial activities, with the evidence mostly coming from inscriptions. They included builders, fullers, shippers, shipbuilders, bakers, wine merchants, and corn measurers. Members of these professions were proud of their work, and their influence. Publius Celerius Amandus had been made a decurion in Ostia by special decree when he was only 18 (he should have been at least 25). His premature death resulted in a detailed tombstone that itemized his short career and also depicted the tools of his trade: two oars, an adze, and a pair of dividers. The shipbuilders were important. Those on the guild roll based at Portus numbered over 350 by the early third century, though this is by no means the largest guild known at Ostia and Portus.

The *collegia* were organized around a formal membership, a constitution of rules, and had a leadership that emulated the civic hierarchy of magistracies. They met in their own dedicated headquarters, the *schola*. In practice membership was often hereditary, and also drew in a member's own freedmen. In this way a guild acted as the commercial link between a patron and his clients. Amandus' father was a freedman; we can assume he too was a shipbuilder and his influence in the guild had brought him civic influence too, and the special privilege granted his son.

Collegia were led by their own class of *magistri*, who were elected to serve for varying periods (usually five years) though the actual numbers of these men serving at any one time varied from guild to guild. They were assisted by elected treasurers. Men who had served as one of these *magistri* were eligible for life status in the position. Freeborn members of guilds were still eligible for civic office. Gnaeus Sentius Felix at Ostia was not only a very senior member of Ostia's town government but also belonged to a guild of shippers and was a patron to many others. The guilds courted the membership of wealthy and powerful men who could offer their members protection and an ear in government, and also fund occasional donations of funds to members or annual celebratory festivals.

Collegia, legal and illegal, certainly existed at Pompeii. The riot in Pompeii's amphitheatre in AD 59 was promptly followed by senatorial sanctions that included the compulsory dissolution of illicit *collegia*. Evidently the *collegia* had played an important part in organizing the violence towards the visiting Nucerians, perhaps founded on simmering commercial rivalries and settling scores. One of the most incongruous figures in the world of Pompeii's guilds is Eumachia. Her imposing building beside the forum reflects how many structures associated with guilds enjoyed prestige locations and the patronage of wealthy individuals, though details of her relationship with the guild of fullers are unknown (see Chapter 3).

Slaves

Patronage even stretched down as far as the slaves. Pompeii had a college of *Ministri Augusti*, another manifestation of the imperial cult. This organization was open both to slaves and freedmen and also had direct links to Pompeii's council. Two slaves, Narcissus and Nymphodotus, serving *ministri* in the cult, made a dedication on the orders of the decurions that probably commemorated an event in the imperial family at the end of first century BC (*CIL* x.908; Ward-Perkins and Claridge no. 206). Other inscriptions show slaves making dedications alongside free men (CC E31). In Pompeii as elsewhere, a reliable slave might in time have hoped for freedom as a reward. If the family that freed him was well-to-do, he could expect to be supported in business. The most successful could live to see their sons reach public office. In many respects our modern sense of 'freedom' and 'slavery' are difficult to reconcile with the far more fluid and blurred meanings of these concepts in the Roman world.

Chapter 3

Public Institutions and Identity

The forum, basilica and attendant buildings

The present form of Pompeii's forum and its associated structures largely dates from the city's growth in the second century BC. Certainly by the beginning of the first century BC the forum had been laid out as an open, rectangular piazza with a two-storey colonnade around the two long sides and the south short side (see Fig. 3.1). The north side was overlooked by the Temple of Jupiter (with Juno and Minerva – the *Capitolium*), an essential piece of political allegiance to Rome's guardian god and father of her destiny. Close by this temple was the market place (*macellum*) and at the south-west corner was the basilica (see below). More buildings were added around the forum in succeeding years and these include a trio of civic government buildings opposite the temple of Jupiter. The centre of these three structures, individually the smallest in the forum area, may have been the council assembly building (*curia*) and was probably flanked by offices for the *duoviri* and the *aediles*, though their identification is uncertain. Pompeii's forum and its surrounding buildings were severely damaged in the earthquake of AD 62, and possibly again by subsequent tremors. In 79 work was underway to rebuild it on an even more impressive scale, probably funded by both wealthy locals and the state.

Ostia's forum straddles the city's main thoroughfare and like Pompeii is also overlooked by a *Capitolium*, though here the temple sits on a far higher podium and faced a temple of Rome and Augustus at the southern end. Public buildings here seem to be confined to the west side with a structure identified as possibly the assembly building for the *curia*, and the basilica. The approximate location of Herculaneum's forum can only be estimated from the remains of its basilica, which is still largely buried. However, one of the nearby buildings was the *Collegium Augustalium*, or headquarters of the imperial cult. It was an appropriately prominent location for the freedmen priests for whom membership was such an important part of their status (Fig. 2.5).

The forum area was in every sense a public area. This was where business, political and social affairs were conducted and where temporary stalls could be set up. It was the centre of gossip, public business and even entertainment. Before the amphitheatre was built the forum acted as a venue for games and gladiatorial displays. The forum was a perfect showcase for the achievements and gifts of the local worthies. Aulus Umbricius Scaurus operated a successful fish sauce (*garum*) concern in Pompeii. The Umbricii had been established at Pompeii since the early first century BC and may have been involved in the *garum* trade for generations. He made no known effort to enter local politics. It was his son of the same name who became a magistrate and who earned public honours when he died unexpectedly young. As a *duumvir* Scaurus the younger was important enough for him to be voted an equestrian statue to be displayed in the forum as recorded on his tomb, and money for his funeral (CC F91, Fig. 5.2). The statue itself is unknown and was perhaps either removed after the earthquake of AD 62 to protect it while repair work was underway, or salvaged soon after the eruption of 79.

A number of other statue bases in the forum record Pompeian *duoviri*, and were probably awarded posthumously also (see Fig. 2.3). In general these were given by decree of the decurions but the opportunity was also there for other organizations to pay their respects. An unspecified rural district near Pompeii set up a statue to the *duumvir* Marcus Holconius Celer, brother or son(?) of Marcus Holconius Rufus, one of the town's most prominent citizens, to show its allegiance to the men who mattered (CC F96).

The basilica

The Roman basilica was a rectangular building with central nave, flanked by aisles and separated from them by rows of columns, and with a recess or apse at one end. It provided a large space for assemblies, and a focal point for those presiding over meetings. The basilica was used as a meeting place for businessmen, a law court where cases were heard and legal records stored, and also for social contact. The design was adapted centuries later for Christian churches.

Pompeii's basilica lies at the south-west corner of the forum (Fig. 3.1). It was probably built around 120-100 BC (a graffito dated to 78 BC proves it was in existence by then) but traces of an earlier building, possibly an earlier basilica, have been found underneath. Visitors entered through one of five main doors at the forum end of the building and found themselves looking down a nave around 55 metres long and 24 metres wide with a raised tribunal at the far end. There were also two small side entrances in the middle of the two long walls. The roof was supported by ten-metre-high brick columns faced with plaster. Little of the building's decoration remains today, but it would have contained statues of emperors, imperial

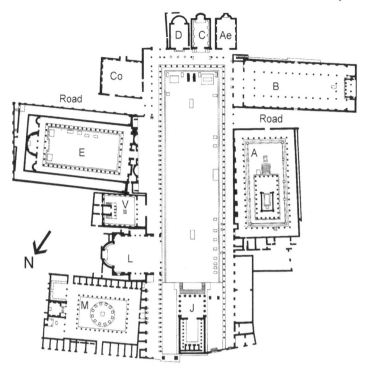

3.1. Pompeii: plan of the Forum. A = temple of Apollo, B = Basilica, Ae = office of the *aediles*(?), C = council chamber(?), D = office of the *duoviri*(?), Co = voting hall(?), E = Building of Eumachia, V = temple of Vespasian/Imperial Cult, L = temple of the city Lares, M = *macellum*, J = Temple of Jupiter.

officials connected with the town, and prominent local men. The walls were stuccoed and painted in the First Style (see p. 66).

One of Pompeii's largest and tallest buildings, the basilica was susceptible to damage from earthquakes. The roof appears to have been destroyed in the earthquake of AD 62 and it is likely that it was still roofless in 79. More severe damage was caused by the eruption but much of the superstructure probably remained visible above the volcanic debris, and was easily carted off by salvage parties in antiquity.

Herculaneum's basilica remains buried but exploration of the site through tunnels in the eighteenth century and more recent tentative explorations have given us a better idea of its original appearance. After an earthquake in the late first century BC the building was repaired by the wealthy and powerful proconsul Marcus Nonius Balbus, who found in the seaside town an opportunity to act as patron and to enjoy the respect that resulted. The civic authorities at Herculaneum repaid his generosity by filling the basilica with statues of Balbus and his family (recovered by the early tunnellers) and naming it the *Basilica Noniana*.

The towns also had other dedicated buildings or complexes devoted to commerce. Pompeii's forum had a *macellum* or market building at its north-east corner, near the Temple of Jupiter and the enigmatic Building of Eumachia. Ostia had what is now called the Piazza of the Corporations.

The Piazza of the Corporations (Ostia II.7.4)

The so-called Piazza of the Corporations is a large colonnaded square behind the theatre in Ostia, and was built at the same time under Augustus (27 BC-AD 14). It covers around 8400 square metres. Alterations took place under Claudius (41-54), Hadrian (117-138), and Septimius Severus (193-211). Around the square are three wings (west, north and east). A small temple, probably dedicated to Ceres, goddess of grain, was built in the late first century AD.

Sixty-one small rooms open off the colonnade. In front of most are mosaics illustrating the overseas trade business of the owners or tenants of the rooms. Many of them depict images associated with the corn trade, and North Africa is the most commonly mentioned region, for example Sabratha and Carthage, and Alexandria in Egypt. Others mention rope-sellers, timber-shippers, ivory and oil (Fig. 3.2). Some show Ostia's lighthouse at the mouth of the Claudian harbour. The rooms are small and were probably offices where traders or their representatives (perhaps

3.2. Ostia: Piazza of the Corporations, mosaic depicting a ship and an inscription stating this is a grain shipping company from *Carales* in Sardinia.

freedmen) could process orders. The imperial procurator in charge of the grain supply would have found it convenient to be able to contact so many traders in one place. So it is possible that the Piazza of the Corporations was under imperial control.

The corporations may have used the square for displays and parades, perhaps on religious festivals associated with Ceres and other deities associated with the goods they dealt in. They certainly took part in imperial parades displaying their banners (*vexilla collegiorum*) under Gallienus (253-268) and Aurelian (270-275) in Rome. The Piazza of the Corporations was originally decorated with statues commemorating prominent Ostian citizens. These included imperial officials, presidents of Ostian guilds, and other local worthies. For example Quintus Calpurnius Modestus, imperial procurator of the corn supply, was honoured with a statue set up by decree of the 'Corporation of Corn Merchants' who had probably benefited from contracts issued by Modestus. Another procurator of the corn supply, Publius Bassilius Crescens, ordered his secretary (*cornicularius*) to hand out gifts in kind to the Corporation of Builders when they dedicated a statue to him.

The Building of Eumachia
One of the most notable figures in the world of Pompeii's commercial corporations (*collegia*) was Eumachia, a businesswoman in her own right, and thus an incongruous figure in Roman society. Her building is the largest structure beside Pompeii's forum (Fig. 3.3). Built in the early first

3.3. Pompeii: the remains of the *chalcidicum* (porch) of the Building of Eumachia, bearing fragments of the dedicatory inscription in her name and that of her son, Marcus Numistrius Fronto.

3.4. Pompeii: one of the inscriptions recording the erection of the Building in Eumachia's name, that of her son Marcus Numistrius Fronto, and its features: the *chalcidicum*, *crypta* and *porticus*. Augustus had built a *chalcidium* on the front of Rome's Senate House (*Res Gestae*, App. 2).

century AD it faces the forum but its southern side wall flanks the main commercial thoroughfare that linked the western and eastern parts of the city (Fig. 3.1). Eumachia was the daughter of Lucius Eumachius who is known from name-stamp impressions to have manufactured brick, wine amphorae and presumably also the wine they contained, in the Pompeii region. His products have been found in North Africa, Gaul and Spain, showing that he was a rich and important businessman. This is likely to have been the source of at least part of her wealth.

Two inscriptions, over the front and back entrances, state Eumachia to have been a public priestess and responsible in her own name and that of her son, Marcus Numistrius Fronto, for the building with its entrance porch (*chalcidicum*) from the forum, covered walkway (*crypta*) and colonnaded walkway (*porticus*) (Fig. 3.4; CC E42). The inscriptions also stated that the building was dedicated to Augustan Concord and Piety. From this we can deduce that the Marcus Numistrius Fronto who was *duumvir* of Pompeii in AD 3 was her husband and that he must have died by the time the building was commissioned or executed, an event thought to postdate AD 10. By associating her son with the building, Eumachia labelled him also as a benefactor to Roman society. This was intended to ensure his future standing and political status in Pompeii. Appropriately for Eumachia's status, her tomb was one of the most extravagant known at Pompeii (see Chapter 5).

A visitor from the forum passed through a portico to be greeted by a façade decorated with niches containing statues of Aeneas and Romulus, linking both Eumachia and her building with Roman traditions, echoing similar arrangements in the Forum of Augustus in Rome. A doorway through the façade led to a large open court surrounded by a two-storied colonnade with a much larger apse at the far end probably housing a statue of Livia (wife of Augustus) with Concord and Piety. Behind that is a further niche containing a statue of Eumachia dedicated by the fullers (CC E43). The fulling trade was one of Pompeii's most important commercial activities, but details of Eumachia's connection with the fullers are unknown. Perhaps her husband had been their patron and perhaps they had supported his candidacy to be a *duumvir*. A number of guild inscriptions from Ostia record women known as *mater* (mother) and *filia* (daughter), possibly because they were wives or daughters of guild *magistri* or patrons. This might explain how Eumachia became associated with the fullers.

The Eumachia building is too elaborate to have been used for the mundane trade of the fullers. Instead it may have been partly honorific and used on particular occasions by the corporation to celebrate their own religious festivals. It may also have been a repository of records and a meeting place for the owners of the respective fulling businesses. Other suggestions include a cloth market, or even a slave market. Another possibility is that the portico and the crypt were used by the guild, while cloth was auctioned, sold and exchanged under the porch in the forum. The building today is not well-preserved. The upper levels are lost and it seems from repairs to the external walls that it had suffered badly in the earthquake of AD 62. Extensive repair work was under way in 79, perhaps funded by the council or by the family of Gnaeus Alleius Nigidius Maius which seems to have had connections with Eumachia, who must have been long dead by then (see Chapter 5).

Entertainment and leisure: theatres and amphitheatres

Civic funds were available for the magistrates to pay for public entertainments, but they were also obliged to pay for some of the events themselves. In addition, theatres were places to be seen in too, where prestige dedicated seating was provided for the great and good by decree of the decurions.

The theatre, with its hemispherical tiers of seats facing the orchestra and stage, was a Greek idea established in Italy by the Greek colonists. Pompeii's theatre was built during the second century BC, well before Rome's first permanent stone theatre, as a direct consequence of the Greek influence in southern Italy. But the theatre was steadily absorbed into Roman tradition, taking on its own identity with a new Latin canon of tragedies and comedies, and inextricably linked with the cycle of religious festivals.

By Augustus' time Pompeii's theatre provided an opportunity for the powerful and wealthy Holconii family to bestow their favours on the city by commissioning a freedman architect called Marcus Artorius Primus to design improvements. An upper seating area was added, along with boxes over the side entrances, and seating for Pompeii's elite in the lower rows of seats and in the orchestra, recorded in an inscription which credits the work to Marcus Holconius Rufus and Marcus Holconius Celer (CC D51). The Holconii were perhaps also reflecting new laws brought in by the Senate in Rome where it had been decreed that senators would have the front row of seats, and that representatives of Rome's allies would no longer be entitled to sit in the orchestra (Suetonius, *Augustus* 44). It seems likely that the Pompeian elite might very well have decided they ought to accord their own magistrates and councillors similar priorities.

In return for this act of generosity, a seating area for Marcus Holconius Rufus was marked out in the theatre with bronze letters around 1 BC (CC D53). A *bisellium* may have been set up here either for actual use by him or posthumously to commemorate his gift. This was certainly what happened at Herculaneum, where the town's patron, Marcus Nonius Balbus, also in the late first century BC, was honoured with a posthumous *bisellium* at the theatre. Balbus was also represented in the theatre by a statue portraying him as a Greek hero, alongside others depicting members of the imperial family and more of Herculaneum's most important citizens. Ostia's theatre, though a more modest affair than Pompeii's, seems to have been paid for by the emperors rather than local worthies. Built originally under Augustus, it was enlarged and improved by Septimius Severus and Caracalla, his son and co-emperor, in AD 196.

Theatres were places where works of great literature could be performed, but the magistrates who paid for the entertainment were aware that the general public had less refined tastes. The kind of shows put on in Roman theatres were increasingly aimed at pleasing the largest possible crowds, and that meant farces, musical shows including comedy and satire, and dance shows that bore some comparison to a combination of ballet and charades. Appropriately enough, actors were officially considered dubious and were excluded from holding public office. Nevertheless, actors were popular amongst their public, especially if they were successful enough to be able to contribute to the town coffers. Gaius Norbanus Sorex, an actor of minor roles, was honoured by the presidents of the Augustan Suburban Country District outside Pompeii with a bronze bust (a 'herm') of himself in the precinct of the Temple of Isis (CC D70).

The small theatre, or odeon, at Pompeii was added immediately next to the large theatre in the first decade after the city's elevation to the status of a Roman colony in 80 BC. It may even have served as the council chamber. It was evidently part of a programme of public works since the *duoviri* in charge of the project, Gaius Quinctius Valgus and Marcus Porcius, also took charge of Pompeii's amphitheatre in the far south-eastern corner of the settlement (see Fig. 3.5, Selected Inscriptions, and CC B9). The difference was that they paid for the amphitheatre out of their own pockets, identifying, apparently correctly, that the Pompeian colonists would be enthusiastic audiences for gladiatorial bouts. The tomb of Aulus Clodius Flaccus records that he celebrated his second duumvirate at Pompeii in Augustan times by putting on a show of fighters in the forum on the first day and a series of gladiatorial bouts and other events in the amphitheatre on the second day (CC D8).There are also the remarkable displays of graffiti and other painted announcements recording forthcoming bouts in the amphitheatre with details of the participants and dates. The interest Pompeii's governing classes had in these events is clear from some of these announcements, and from other monuments. Aulus Suettius Certus was an *aedile* in Neronian times at Pompeii and had his own band of gladiators whose forthcoming appearances were publicized in the city (CC D16). The tomb of the *aedile* Gaius Vestorius Priscus has paintings of gladiatorial bouts, perhaps a record of ones he had put on during his election campaign or while in office (see Fig. 2.2, and also Chapter 5).

Gnaeus Alleius Nigidius Maius, *quinquennalis* in AD 55-56, was a regular impresario in the last two decades of Pompeii's life and was feted by a grateful Pompeian as *princeps munerariorum*, 'chief of the gladiatorial show exhibitors'. Nigidius Maius' run of popularity risked coming to an abrupt end in 59 when the riot broke out in the amphitheatre and led to a ten-year senatorial ban on further gladiatorial fights at Pompeii (see Chapter 1). The enterprising Nigidius Maius put on an athletics show, a hunt, and a procession in the amphitheatre instead so that he could maintain his popularity with the Pompeian public (CC D21-2).

As in the theatre, seating areas in the amphitheatre with the best views were set aside for the most important people. These seats were accessed through a tunnel that meant the magistrates and the other elite could enter without having to mingle with the crowd. Ordinary spectators had to climb the amphitheatre's external stairways, enter through the top and then walk down one of the stairways that divided the seating area. A solid wall ran round the middle of the seating area to separate the elite from the crowd.

So far as we know Ostia had no amphitheatre, but this did not prevent the staging of gladiatorial shows. Publius Lucius Gamala, a member of a family whose members frequently held office in Ostia, gave a gladiatorial display in the mid-second century, perhaps in the basilica where a show was put on in AD 152, proudly recounting how they had been 'amplified' at his own expense. The town has little in the way of open areas where large-scale events could be put on. The forum, for example, is much smaller than Pompeii's. The most likely possibility is that Ostia had an amphitheatre outside the walls, perhaps made of timber. However, in 2009 an amphitheatre was discovered in an imperial palace at Portus.

Entertainment and leisure: baths and gymnasia

One of Pompeii's most remarkable features was its combination of Italian and Greek traditions. Next to the theatre is the tiny Samnite *palaestra*, effectively a Greek-style gymnasium, and next to the amphitheatre is the huge open space of the large *palaestra* (Fig. 3.5). Little is known about either, though the large *palaestra* probably belongs to the first century BC or shortly afterwards. The large *quadriportico* which Pompeii's theatre overlooks was a gladiators' barracks in the city's last few years, but may originally have been a public *palaestra*.

The traditional Roman view had been that bathing, a Greek custom, was an effete and decadent habit that washed off the honest grime of farming and military service. But baths had become part of civic life by the late first century BC, as the Roman world became increasingly accustomed to comfort. Physical exercise formed an important preamble to bathing, so it was common to build a *palaestra* at a public baths. Visiting the baths is often said to have most commonly taken place after midday and into the early afternoon. By then the morning court sessions, business and trading activities were over, and the water hot. Much of the afternoon might then be spent at the baths, before returning home or visiting a friend's or a business associate's house for a social gathering. In practice, however, it is unlikely that the Pompeian day was quite so rigidly structured.

A busy town needed several bathing establishments. Different baths were presumably frequented by the patrons and clients of different civic

3.5. Pompeii: the amphitheatre, and beyond the large *palaestra*. The amphitheatre was built shortly after 80 BC in the extreme south-east of the city on a site cleared of houses to make way for it (see p. 114).

factions. They provided perfect venues for transacting business, conspiring and negotiating. Here men could relax with their peers, friends, and clients after the day's work. Women bathed in separate facilities, as in Pompeii's forum and Stabian Baths, or at different times.

Baths were free or could cost as little as a *quadrans*, the smallest denomination coin, because they were heavily subsidized. Providing or improving baths was one of the main options the magistrates had for spending town funds. Soon after Pompeii became a colony in 80 BC, the town-centre Stabian Baths were upgraded by the *duoviri* Caius Uulius and Publius Aninius (CC B11). This is a very early example of the obligations placed on the new colony's magistrates. They opted to spend the money which they were compelled to spend on public entertainment or building on rebuilding the porticoes and the *palaestra*, as well as adding sweating and scraping room facilities. This important contribution to civic life was proudly commemorated on an inscription.

Pompeii's Forum Baths were built from scratch around the same time or a little later. They were conveniently located behind the Temple of Jupiter. The *duoviri* of AD 3-4 had a marble washing basin installed at a cost to the city of 5,250 sesterces (CC D106). The statement of the cost was perhaps both an attempt to show how much money the council was prepared to spend on public facilities, as well as to show a degree of accountability: 'this is what your money was spent on'.

The general impression from Pompeii's housing stock is of an increasing population density in the city's last few years, which would have increased demand for civic facilities. This would help explain the construction of a brand new baths complex by the next main crossroads north of the Stabian Baths. The new 'Central Baths' were still under construction in AD 79. The baths had yet to be fitted with decorations, and the drainage system had not been completed, but they included technical innovations such as hollow box-flue tiles in the walls and large glazed windows. Its prominent location suggests that it was a civic initiative, perhaps underwritten at least in part by a wealthy benefactor as well as by civic funds.

Baths could be privately-funded establishments, such as those owned by Marcus Crassus Frugi (see below). The astonishingly well-preserved Suburban Baths at Herculaneum were built on a terrace below Herculaneum's main level and overlooked the seashore. They may have been built by the owner of the House of the Relief of Telephus which lies just above and behind the baths, and had its own private access to the building. The baths themselves have been tentatively dated to the 40s or early 50s AD. This is too late for Marcus Nonius Balbus, whose statue and tomb stand in the square outside close to the baths' entrance. It is possible that

his family were responsible, though no inscription has survived to sub-
stantiate this theory (see Figs 2.1 and 3.6, B).

The square was extremely busy, as it was one of the main routes down
to the boatyards by the sea. The door into the baths is framed by two half
columns and a pediment (see Fig. 2.1). This seems to have been largely
bricked up during the baths' lifetime in order to create a much smaller
entrance. From here the bather went downstairs into a hall designed like
a small atrium with four columns supporting pairs of arches beneath a
skylight (Fig. 3.6 right, A). A herm of Apollo on a pedestal between two
of the columns poured water from a fountain into a basin below the
skylight (Fig. 3.6 left). Beyond lay the baths themselves (Fig. 3.6 right).
The *tepidarium* (warm room, T) and *caldarium* (hot room, C) overlooked
the sea. The *frigidarium* (cold room, F) lay inside the building along with

3.6. Herculaneum: the Suburban Baths. Opposite: *atrium* with herm doubling as a fountain, *c.* AD 40. Right: plan. D = probable *diaeta* (waiting room). For other rooms see the main text. B marks the site of the piazza with the statue and tomb of Marcus Nonius Balbus (see Fig. 2.1).

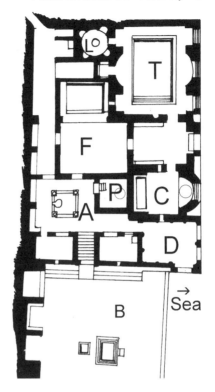

the *praefurnium* (furnace, P) and *laconicum* (sweat room, L). There was only one suite of baths which meant it was either men-only, or was used alternately by men and women. The building was extensively decorated with stucco figures of warriors, cupids, and motifs, marble wall panels, floors, and seating. There was no *palaestra*, since there was no room for one. Some of the baths' wooden doors, wood fuel for the furnace and working plumbing components have been preserved.

The building's survival virtually intact is probably due to the massive concrete construction and the use of skylights which allowed volcanic debris to fill the rooms at the same time as it accumulated outside, thus equalizing the pressure. The *caldarium* preserves a large marble basin which was flung across the room when the pyroclastic surge of super-heated volcanic mud surged down from Vesuvius and buried the city.

At Ostia bathing establishments began to appear on a significant scale from the early first century AD on. In the second century, as Ostia reached its commercial climax, more baths were built and this continued into the fourth century. Unlike at Pompeii, inscriptions testify to imperial funding.

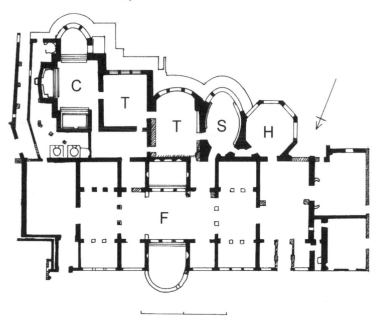

3.7. Ostia: plan of the Forum Baths. F = *Frigidarium* (cold room), C = *Caldarium* (hot room), T = *Tepidaria* (warm rooms), S = *Sudatorium* (sweat room), H = *Heliocaminos* (sun room). Mid-second century AD.

The Baths of Neptune were built with two million sesterces provided by Hadrian and additional funds supplied by his successor, Antoninus Pius. However, fire damage was made good by Publius Lucilius Gamala, one of Ostia's great private benefactors.

The Forum Baths are the largest baths in Ostia (Fig. 3.7). The main sequence of baths occupies the north wing of an irregularly shaped *insula* and overlooks a triangular *palaestra* with a small temple. The main western entrance faced the forum. The main northern block, which houses the *frigidarium*, is symmetrical but along its southern flank are the heated rooms with large windows which protrude into the *palaestra* in staggered form from east to west, with the eastern rooms protruding the furthest. This maximized the amount of sunshine entering the rooms in the later part of the day, the traditional time for visiting them, but also dramatically enhanced the appearance of the baths from the forum. Without this feature, the heated rooms would have been obscured by the mass of the *frigidarium* block to anyone heading towards the baths from the forum. The effect would have been to make the baths seem bigger and more impressive rather than leaving them lurking behind the *frigidarium*. The person or institution responsible for the baths is unknown. A fragmentary inscription suggests that the baths were built by Marcus Gavius Maximus, praetorian prefect (one of the highest posts open to the equestrian class) under Antoninus Pius (AD 138-161).

The much smaller Baths of Mithras, towards the western end of town, occupy an irregular rectangular plot. Probably provided by private benefaction in the second century AD under Hadrian, they represent part of the extensive rebuilding of this area of Ostia begun under Trajan. Two carved portrait busts in roundels, *imagines clipeatae*, presumably represent a now-anonymous husband and wife who funded the baths. The baths have two particularly interesting features. The well-preserved service area has fittings for a waterwheel used to raise water for use in the baths because Ostia's aqueducts were unable to cope with the increase in demand when the city went through its explosive second-century growth. Underneath the western side of the baths is a mithraeum. The latter reflects the nature of a male-dominated trading population and worship here is likely to have been closely linked to the users of the baths. It was not built before the end of the second century. The Baths of Mithras seem to have fallen out of use by the fourth century. The heating facilities had been abandoned and a Christian oratory installed. It is possible the old baths were now used as baptism fonts.

Private baths were only installed in Pompeii's largest houses, and were even rarer in Ostia where the extensive public facilities made them unnecessary. Private baths in any case almost by definition lacked the essential social qualities and opportunities of the public baths. At Ostia, the House of the Dioscures in its fourth-century form had its own baths but was unique in this respect; all the other late grand houses lacked baths, their owners presumably content to use public baths. Nevertheless, since public baths were open to almost anyone, it is no surprise, in a world where status was eagerly sought and proudly displayed, that more exclusive facilities were available. This seems to have been the case with the private Baths of Julia Felix, advertised as being let only to people of a certain status (see p. 24). The Baths of Marcus Crassus Frugi lay outside Pompeii and have not been found; they are known only from an inscription advertising them (CC D109). Operated by his freedman Januarius, both freshwater and seawater baths were available, probably on an exclusive basis to suitable clients. Crassus Frugi belonged to a Roman family of senatorial rank and this man may have been the one who was consul in AD 64.

Religion and social status

The most conspicuous evidence of religious activity in Roman towns is provided by the state cults, principally their temples. At Ostia the *Capitolium*, dedicated to Jupiter (and Juno and Minerva), faced south across the forum to the temple of Rome and Augustus. The latter was built under Tiberius (AD 14-37) but the *Capitolium* was rebuilt under Hadrian (117-138). At Pompeii the Temple of Jupiter looked down across the forum from the north. Pompeii's temple of Apollo lay beyond the western wall of the forum and just beyond that and behind the basilica was the temple dedicated to the town's patron goddess, Venus (Fig. 3.1). All of these were badly damaged in AD 62.

The rituals of the state cults were performed according to a strict cycle of events in the annual religious calendar, and were statements of political loyalty to Rome. Taking part was also how men of substance exhibited their status in the town and their allegiance to the state. They belonged to priestly colleges, to which they had been appointed or elected. Being a priest was a role that they adopted as part of a portfolio of civic honours, just as Augustus was *pontifex maximus* ('chief priest') at Rome. At Pompeii by the end of the first century BC Marcus Lucretius Decidianus Rufus had been a *duumvir* three times, and also a priest, *pontif(ex)*, recorded on a statue base that commemorated his career (Fig. 2.3; CC F92). This was yet another example of how a provincial town emulated the goings-on in Rome. The senator Pliny the Younger, in the early second century, basked in the honour of being made an *augur*, a priestly interpreter of omens, by Trajan (AD 98-117). It was another achievement to add to his status as a member of Rome's elite (*Letters* iv.8.1) as it was for Decidianus Rufus to be a priest at Pompeii as part of his membership of the Pompeian elite. As a woman Eumachia was denied political status but by being made a *sacerdos publica* ('public priestess') her membership of an influential and successful family could take on a more formal role. Alleia, daughter of Nigidius Maius, Pompeii's most successful gladiatorial impresario, was made a priestess in the cult of Venus and Ceres (CC E49).

Marcus Tullius was a notable Pompeian at the beginning of the first century AD. His career as a magistrate was similar to that of Decidianus Rufus, but he had been made an *augur*. Tullius owned land in the heart of Pompeii, immediately across the road from the Forum Baths, and only a few metres north of the temple of Jupiter. He decided to donate some of his land on this prime site for a new temple of Augustan Fortune. Tullius advertised his generosity on an inscription that recorded how he had provided the land and the funds (CC E32). The administration of the temple remained under civic control; several inscriptions record how decrees of the decurions had ordered magistrates to supervise the erection of a statue by the cult attendants.

The Temple of Jupiter (Capitolium)

Jupiter, equal to the Greek Zeus, was Rome's guardian god. The classical-style Temple of Jupiter at Pompeii was a focal point in formal religious ceremonies, and dominated the forum. It was built in the second century BC while Pompeii was still a Samnite city. After Pompeii was made a Roman colony the temple was rededicated to the Roman Capitoline Triad: Jupiter Optimus Maximus Capitolinus (part of whose cult statue survives), his wife Juno, and his daughter (born from Jupiter's brain) Minerva, the goddess of wisdom, war and liberal arts. The *cella* was divided into three chambers to accommodate them. In AD 62 the temple was severely damaged by the earthquake and may have suffered from subsequent tremors. In 79 the temple was still under repair, partly explaining its poor state of preservation today though it is also likely that part of its superstructure was timber. Building inscriptions from the temple had presumably been removed after the earthquake of 62, leaving us without any detailed information. This is in direct contrast to the Temple of Isis, which had been repaired by 79 and about which we know considerably more.

However, between AD 47 and 54 the town councillors voted for space in the temple for a statue of Spurius Turranius Proculus Gellianus, whose career had included a number of civilian and military posts as well as serving as a priest of Jupiter, and of Mars (CC E11). Temples also functioned as public art galleries, where the elite could display and commemorate their generosity. Pliny the Younger acquired a Greek bronze statue which he paid for out of a legacy he had received. Rather proud of this new piece he decided to display it in the Temple of Jupiter in *Comum* (Como) and arranged for a marble pedestal with his name and titles inscribed on it (*Letters* iii.6, see pp. 111-12).

The Temple of Isis

Isis was an ancient Egyptian goddess but by the first century BC her worship had evolved into one of the Roman Empire's mystery cults. These cults, which include Christianity and Mithraism, are partly defined by their belief in a religious process that involved a transition to higher awareness of divine power, allied to a belief in rebirth and an afterlife, generally through a process of initiation. Isis emerged as a goddess associated with a number of other female goddesses like Demeter and

3.8. Pompeii: Temple of Isis. The kiosk just visible on the left housed purifying water in a well. Built in this form AD 62-79.

Aphrodite, whose identities she subsumed, and deities like Dionysus. Since in ancient Egyptian mythology Isis had resurrected her dead husband Osiris, her transition to being a Roman goddess of rebirth was an easy one to make. Isis was popular in Pompeii and statuettes of her have been found in a number of household shrines.

The temple of Isis is sited at a prime location immediately behind Pompeii's theatre. Immediately to the east is another temple, thought originally to have been dedicated to Jupiter Milichius ('Gracious Jupiter', the patron of farmers) and now believed to have been dedicated to Aesculapius, the god of healing. The more important temple of Isis is a compact structure built on an approximately square podium divided equally between a colonnaded portico and a *cella* facing east (Fig. 3.8). It was reached by steps and sat in the centre of a walled precinct with a rectangular colonnade. The colonnaded enclosure contained altars dedicated to Harpocrates and Anubis and also a small booth containing a water tank which was used during the purification ritual. The precinct was enclosed by a solid external wall but the zone between the wall and colonnade was used to display a number of statues including Isis, Venus and Bacchus. To the west doors allowed access to a meeting hall and initiation chamber. To the south-east were rooms for the priests. The structure as it survives dates to the rebuilding after the earthquake of 62, and replaced an earlier temple tentatively dated to the mid-first century BC. Isis had probably been worshipped in Pompeii soon after she was introduced to nearby Puteoli in 105 BC.

Isis-worship initially provoked official disquiet in Rome, but by the first century AD the cult had become mainstream. Indeed, it was the process of restoration work which meant that in 79 the Temple of Isis, unlike that of Jupiter, was in a fairly complete state. Appropriate to its date, it had Fourth-Style painting (see Chapter 4) on its walls depicting Isis and other Egyptian deities such as Osiris, Bes and Anubis, set in Egyptian landscapes. Hieroglyphic texts were also found carved on a slab by the temple steps. During excavation traces of burnt sacrificial gifts were found on the altar, and offerings of foodstuffs such as figs and nuts buried in pits in the precinct.

That the probable freedman Numidius Popidius Ampliatus was able to buy his six-year-old son a place as a decurion by paying for post-earthquake repairs to the temple suggests it was town property, as does Lucius Caecilius Phoebus' donation of a statue of Isis on a spot in the precinct given 'by decree of the decurions' (CC C5, E5, pp. 113-14). The Caecilii are well-known as a family of bankers in Pompeii, who presumably sought public recognition of their status. Ampliatus' personal involvement is shown by his dedication of a statue of Bacchus as Osiris found in the temple (CC E4). An unusual inclusion in the precinct was a bust of the actor Norbanus Sorex, who perhaps had helped fund either the temple's restoration or the cult.

Given such connections it is unsurprising that the Isis-worshippers were a political force in Pompeii. Several electoral notices were painted close by. One announces that 'all the Isis-worshippers' (*Isiaci universi*) were supporting Gnaeus Helvius Sabinus to be elected as *aedile*. Sabinus, we may assume, was one of the Isis-worshippers. Once more we see the system of patronage with the candidacy of Cuspius Pansa to be *aedile*. The Isis-worshippers supported him along with his client Popidius Natalis, a man who we can be sure was either another member of the same prominent and important Pompeian Popidii family that might have freed Numidius Popidius Ampliatus (assuming he was a freedman) or was another of its freedmen (CC E7-8).

*

Although Roman towns had many similar facilities, the public entertainment and religious buildings being the most conspicuous, they often also had unique features. Ostia was an unusual town with exceptional needs, and it therefore had important structures not usually found elsewhere.

Ostia: Firefighters' Barracks

The barracks of the *vigiles* in Ostia reflects the town's unique blend of local officialdom and the imperial interest in keeping the place safe and secure. It was a practical precaution. Grain, in hot and dry storage buildings, could easily catch fire in a trivial accident. No sensible emperor could afford to risk the grain supply. Claudius was mobbed when drought caused shortages (Suetonius, *Claudius* 18.2). He took measures to maintain shipments and also 'stationed a cohort at Puteoli and one at Ostia to protect against the misfortune of fires' (ibid. 25.2). The headquarters of the *vigiles* was built *c.* AD 117-138, and restored in 207. Inscriptions from the building cease by 244, suggesting that the firefighters had been transferred to the increasingly important Portus (Fig. 3.9). The firefighters were emphatically under imperial control. This was not a building in which local worthies commemorated their gifts to the town or had their generosity and achievements acknowledged by their peers.

Firefighters were sent from the Rome cohorts on four-month tours of duty, changing over on 15 December, 15 April, and 15 August, rotating with Puteoli and Rome. Firefighters received a grant of state corn, and those of Latin status earned full Roman citizenship after three years in the job. The work included all-night patrols armed with axes and buckets, operating a simple fire engine called a *siphon*. Under Vespasian (AD 69-79) an appeal was made for a subsidy to help pay for their footwear. The discipline-conscious emperor responded by ordering that they march

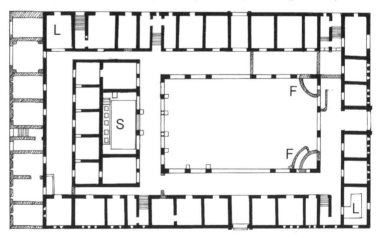

3.9. Ostia: Barracks of the *Vigiles* (firefighters). S = Shrine, L = Latrines, F = Fountains. A number of stairwells are visible, leading to the upper storey(s).

barefoot henceforth, which carried on at least until Suetonius recorded the fact in the early second century (*Vespasian* 8). In AD 168 and 239 there were four centurions, indicating that there were around 320 firefighters (there were 80 men in a Roman military 'century'). The firefighters were commanded by one or two tribunes. By 211 it seems that all the firefighters had come under a centralized command: the Rome sub-prefect in charge of all the firefighters spent at least part of his term at Ostia.

The plan of the Firefighters' Barracks was a reworking of a design used for courtyard apartment blocks, and also for some of the warehouses (see for example the Great Warehouse). However, it looked almost entirely inwards with only slit windows facing out to the streets. The main entrance was from the east (right on the plan), though there was access from the north and south too. In the middle was an open courtyard surrounded by a portico built on brick piers rather than columns, which was probably used for firefighting exercises, and ceremonies. A series of eighteen rooms surrounded the portico.

The most conspicuous feature of the Firefighters' Barracks is its shrine dedicated to the imperial cult. The western side was dominated by this shrine which faced the eastern entrance. Entering the shrine meant crossing a mosaic depicting a sacrifice of a bull and then going up a step into the shrine. Here remain several inscribed blocks dedicated to Antoninus Pius (138-161), Marcus Aurelius (161-180) and his short-lived co-emperor Lucius Verus (161-169), and Septimius Severus (193-211). The shrine and the inscriptions show the importance of observing a cycle of religious statements of loyalty to the regime, administered by the commanding officers of the barracks.

Ostia: the Great Warehouse

The principal Ostian granaries were probably owned by the emperor and operated by his slaves and freedmen. No inscriptions from Ostia are known referring to workers or managers of the granaries. The original building, built under Claudius (41-54), consisted of four wings of store-rooms arranged around a U-shaped colonnaded courtyard with a further set of storerooms in the middle, and must reflect the increased commercial activity at Ostia and imperial preoccupation with a more reliable grain supply.

It has been calculated that the original Claudian Great Warehouse could accommodate at least 5,660 tonnes of grain, enough to feed perhaps 14,000 people for a year (Hermansen 1981). The building bears quite a close resemblance to the Firefighters' Barracks, and also the apartment blocks. Access was from the north through a portico that faced the quays on the River Tiber a short distance away. The portico, east and west walls, and courtyard columns were made of tufa, the south wall from brick-faced concrete. This was extremely strong and could withstand internal stresses. There were no stairways and no upstairs levels at this time.

Under Nero (54-68) the east and west wings were doubled in size by adding extra rows of externally facing rooms. Over-stocking, however, could cause its own problems. In 62 state grain had been allowed to rot, 'through age'(Tacitus, *Annals* xv.18). This could have been caused both by a lack of suitable building precautions and by a lack of confidence that unexpected shortages could be weathered, after Claudius' experience at the hands of a hungry mob following shortages caused by drought (Suetonius, *Claudius* 18). By the late second century (161-192), the Great Warehouse had been almost completely rebuilt at a higher level, and suspended floors had been installed to protect grain from damp and rodents. Many rooms had been rebuilt in brick. Stairways indicate there was another floor. By the reign of Severus (193-211) the north wing had been rebuilt again and raised, with suspended floors, increasing capacity further. Now there was only one narrow entrance in the north wall. Arches and piers were added to support the south wall. Arches, and a possible fire escape, crossed the road to the west. The Great Warehouse was disused by the late fourth century, reflecting the loss of trade and population to Portus. The building is now largely robbed out, giving little impression of its former significance (Fig. 3.10).

Fig. 3.10. Ostia, the Great Warehouse.

Chapter 4

Private Expressions of Social Identity

The size of the Roman private house, its location in the town, its fittings and decorations, and the presence or lack of other businesses or residences within the same *insula* all helped define the status of the owner and his or her wealth. Visitors to the House of the Menander in Pompeii were greeted by a skilfully-designed visual axis right through the house to the painted *exedra* on the far side of the peristyle, disguising the house's asymmetrical lay-out (see Fig. 1.4). On the face of it, such houses appear to have clearly-defined areas for receiving guests, private rooms and working or service zones, but it is clear from artefacts and other finds that space was used according to requirements. At the other end of the scale were the occupants of small apartments let out in parts of the large Pompeian *insulae* and, at Ostia in the second century AD, the residents of apartment blocks that proliferated throughout the town during its commercial climax.

The Roman day
Martial's description of the Roman day is the main source of our information, though it is by no means the only one (*Epigrams* iv.8.1-6). In his account, the first two hours involved householders greeting their clients who waited outside their houses, before heading off to the forum, basilica or other public buildings to deal with their business or public affairs for the rest of the morning. Work wound down by noon, followed by a midday meal and rest before heading to the baths and gymnasia for the first part of the afternoon. The late afternoon saw people heading back to their homes for the main meal of the day in the very late afternoon and early evening.

Not all Pompeians or Ostians would have rigidly followed this pattern of activities every day. The reality must have depended on circumstance, opportunity, needs, and unexpected turns of events. It was also a question of status. A wealthy householder might have the luxury of greeting his clients at home, but his clients of course had already been up and about and made a journey to their patron's house.

The traditional *atrium* house (*domus*)

Roman private houses included certain basic features that make them resemble homes from any time: rooms for sleeping, rooms for entertaining, and utility areas. However, the traditional Roman atrium townhouse was almost completely inward-facing. External walls gave almost no hint of the house within and were broken up only by the doorways to rental accommodation in peripheral parts of the *insulae* or shop fronts. The only signs of an important house were the doorway and the benches outside where clients waited on their patron. Electoral slogans and other painted notices might refer to the owner and his interests, but there was little sense of a house having any kind of external architectural pretensions apart from the doorway's designs. The expressions of status lay within.

Only at Pompeii, Herculaneum and Ostia do many Roman private houses survive together with enough evidence to help us understand how they worked. 'Worked' is appropriate – houses were designed to perform tasks. They reflected Roman society in their design and reinforced it by defining public and private space, and zones for the different levels in the domestic hierarchy. No two houses are alike, though most conform to a basic pattern. The differences are mostly in scale. A visitor passed through the main door through a deceptively unimpressive passage (*fauces*, literally 'jaws'). On either side of the entrance there were often rented shops fronting the street. The visitor then reached the *atrium*, a large entrance hall which was lit by a rectangular opening in the roof called a *compluvium*. The roof pitched down on all four sides to the *compluvium*, maximizing the amount of light let in, especially in the earlier and later part of the day. Some large *atria* were embellished with columns to support the roof at each corner of the *compluvium*, but this also recalled the monumental architecture of public buildings and was appropriate to a 'public' part of the house, especially one owned by an important man. Any rainwater was collected in a small rectangular recess in the floor called an *impluvium* (see Fig. 1.4) and drained into an under-floor reservoir. It was in the *atrium* that the household shrine (*lararium*) for the household spirits (*lares*) was usually situated. This hall was emphatically public, but around it were gathered the bedrooms (*cubicula*) for the members of the owning family.

To the northern European the *atrium* seems dingy but it offered essential shade from the blistering heat of the Mediterranean summer sun. This was where the owner of the house conducted the morning *salutatio*, when he accepted calls from his clients, exchanged news with them, received updates about the businesses they operated for him, heard their complaints, told them what he could do to help them and what he expected

4.1. Herculaneum: House of the Wooden Partition. This house retains the wooden screens that separated the *atrium* from the *tablinum*.

from them in return. It was also here that he presided over the daily household religious ceremonies, honouring the *lares*. But it is also clear that the *atrium* and its surrounding rooms could be used for much more mundane activities, including light industry. The use of rooms in the Roman house was not governed by a rule book.

Beyond the *atrium* was the *tablinum*, which usually lay between the *atrium* and the *peristylium* (peristyle) beyond. It acted as the nerve centre of the owner's estate and business. Here he worked with his slaves and freedmen to deal with paperwork recording transactions, leases, contracts and so on. These were all stored in the *tablinum*, secured in a strong box. Structurally, the *tablinum* was open to both the *atrium* and peristyle, but curtains or wooden screens were often available to be pulled across to make it private (Fig. 4.1).

The peristyle was an internal garden surrounded by a covered colonnade. It offered a peaceful open-air refuge from the busy streets outside.

The gardens were carefully laid out and so long as a public water-supply was available (which it was not at Pompeii after AD 62) fountains and pools often formed part of the decorations. The function of individual rooms around the peristyle is not always clear. However, a dining room was frequently located next to the *tablinum* while others probably included further bedrooms and private chambers for family members. Discreet narrow corridors led off to service areas. Slaves, if they were lucky, might have their own cramped quarters but more often simply slept where they could.

This is a very general description and it owes much to Vitruvius as well as observations in the actual houses. In practice, the detail varies considerably. The very largest houses, such as the House of the Faun in Pompeii, often feature duplicated room sequences, but they still conform to the sense of progression. Anyone entering through the *fauces* was able to see through the *atrium*, the *tablinum* (assuming the shutters were not closed) and out to the peristyle beyond. The more imposing the *atrium*, the more distant and more extravagant the peristyle, the more impressive the house was. In Pompeii's House of the Vettii the visitor passes from the principal *atrium* (there were two) directly to the peristyle, which was that house's dominant feature. The House of Sallust, also in Pompeii, retained its standard second-century BC *atrium* suite but by AD 79 the open garden surrounding it had been replaced with more rooms including a modest peristyle accessed awkwardly by a corridor cut through from the *atrium*. By the same date many of the more elaborate houses at Pompeii and Herculaneum had rented out external rooms to shops and businesses, and created self-contained apartments through skilful blocking of walls and installation of upstairs suites.

New building techniques

Ostia's remarkable Garden House complex of the second century AD (see p. 80ff. below) was an attempt to satisfy an affluent market in a different era. Here the developers provided luxury apartments in their own private court. Elsewhere in Ostia more basic apartment blocks rose up to accommodate a growing population during the second century. Both were a response to different circumstances. Whenever urban populations rise, land prices follow and the tendency is to build upwards. The construction of multi-storied blocks increased the availability of accommodation, provided street frontage shops that could be let, and generally maximized the rental yield of each plot. The new technique of building with brick-faced concrete was fast, strong and flexible. The remains of Ostia now seem to consist of the ruins of brick-faced houses, apartment blocks, baths and public buildings.

The new buildings at Ostia reflect the building regulations brought in after Rome's disastrous fire of AD 64. This contrasts with Pompeii and Herculaneum where the housing stock in 79 was still largely made up of much older houses. In Ostia's later years the town became a less overtly commercial centre as business moved to Portus. The late houses show far less concern with visual axes and traditional progressions of rooms based on an *atrium* suite. Instead they made do with what was available, adapting existing structures as desired. The House of the Dioscures shows this to good effect, creating one of Ostia's most luxurious late Roman houses.

Decoration

Decoration played an important part in defining space in the Roman house, what it would be used for and who would use it. Its absence is as significant as its presence. Service areas made little concession to comfort or embellishment. Their walls might be plastered but were usually left plain or painted with simple bands and stripes and their floors were equally plain, usually *opus signinum*. The public rooms, and those used by the immediate members of the owner's family, were treated very differently though this depended on their status, their tastes and wealth. Some wooden couches, seats and beds survive at Herculaneum but these were salvaged or rotted away at Pompeii, leaving only occasional examples of bronze and stone furnishings. Some plaster casts of wooden fittings and furniture have been made. Decorations could enhance the effect of architectural features, or make up for where they were absent. Some of the most imposing *atria* had columns supporting the roof at the corners of the *compluvium* but many did not. It was inevitably a choice based on circumstances and taste and the desire (or lack of it) to make an impression.

Wall-painting

Wall-painting is probably the most conspicuous decoration at Pompeii and Herculaneum today, and to a much lesser extent at Ostia where conditions made its survival less likely. It was a feature of public and religious buildings, but these for the greater part are far less well-preserved (the Temple of Isis being an exception). Moreover, public buildings were more likely to make use of *opus sectile*, marble veneer or stucco imitating marble for their wall decorations. For these reasons wall-painting is a far more important factor in understanding private houses.

Wall-painting had become popular by the second century BC and remained in vogue thereafter. Styles of course changed, and these have been used as an important tool in dating the development of houses at

Pompeii and Herculaneum. This is not necessarily reliable since it was quite possible for a householder to choose either to leave older styles intact or even deliberately to recreate them. The technique was highly skilled and involved applying several layers of plaster to the wall, beginning with coarser layers for grip. The finest layer was usually painted while still wet so that the paint combined with the plaster, creating a more durable finish. Pompeii's House of the Painters at Work (IX.12.9) is so named because it preserves actual work-in-progress; the painters literally downed tools as the eruption started and ran, leaving pots of paint and other equipment behind.

Today, four principal styles are recognized, the first three of which are described by Vitruvius (vii.5). All were normally divided into three zones: a dado about 50-90 cm in height, a main panelled area about 2.5-2.7 m in height and an upper zone which acted as a border between the main scheme and the ceiling. The dates are only an approximation.

The 'First Style' was mostly popular between around 150 and 90 BC. Quite unlike the later styles, it used plaster and paint to imitate solid marble and masonry blocks. The effect was a two-dimensional scheme of different-coloured rectangles and squares in rows along a wall.

The 'Second Style' came into vogue around the time Pompeii became a Roman colony and up to about 25 BC, shortly after Augustus came to power. Second-Style walls have false perspective scenes of three-dimensional buildings, doors, and colonnades, all set in fantasy landscapes to create a sense of depth. The architectural features have a rather overbearing appearance.

Third-Style paintings abandoned attempts at creating realistic architectural views. Instead, paintings of individual landscape or mythical scenes were set in plain-coloured fields divided up by flimsy-looking borders of leaves and ornamental motifs. These designs were common from about 25 BC to AD 40. From c. 40 the Fourth-Style paintings represented an innovative conflation of earlier styles in new designs. The Third-Style painted scenes now found themselves set in more elegant versions of Second-Style fantasy architectural panels. The inspiration for some of the painted scenes probably came from manuals that reproduced the designs by 'old masters' from the Greek world. The vast majority of surviving wall-paintings at Pompeii and Herculaneum are Fourth-Style.

These styles were not unique to Pompeii and Herculaneum. They were also used in Rome. The elite at Pompeii and Herculaneum took their style cues from the capital. But the natural course of development at Rome meant that surviving examples, such as the Second-Style designs in the House of Augustus are rare.

Preservation of older styles, such as some First-Style wall-painting in large parts of the House of the Faun, functioned in the same way as possessing handed-down family antique furniture, or old paintings, might do today. It showed a sense of being established, and might help to differentiate 'old money' from the 'new money' flashed about at Pompeii by the new breed of affluent freedmen who seem to have been busy having their houses painted in the Fourth Style in Pompeii's final years. The Vettii brothers were freedmen and they spent a small fortune on redecorating their home between AD 62 and 79. They ordered wall-paintings that included depictions of mythical scenes copied from Greek originals, and cupids engaged in various trades such as metalworking, echoing Petronius' scathing portrait of the pretentious freedman Trimalchio in the *Satyricon*. Appropriately enough, their principal *atrium* prominently displayed money chests, badges of honour for its prosperous freedmen owners and their commercial interests. At the other end of town the owner of the House of Octavius Quartio used wall paintings to create a learned aura in his dining room and enhance the sense of his garden as a grotto in a fantasy landscape (Fig. 4.6).

Mosaics and other flooring
Mosaic and other decorative floors were also important but they tend to take on a disproportionate level of significance to modern eyes. This is because in most Roman ruins the floor is the only part of the decoration left, if it survives at all, and because many belong to the third and fourth centuries AD when extravagant mosaics were laid in late Roman rural villas. At Pompeii and Herculaneum the floor can be seen as part of an overall decorative ensemble. They were practical too: they could be swept and washed, though they were cold and were damaged by wear and tear. Early mosaics, little known before the mid-first-century BC, tended to be simple black-and-white geometric designs, though it was possible to commission coloured scenes that were set into the floor. These were expensive extras that were made to order in mosaic workshops by using extremely small *tesserae*. They reflect the painted scenes that were a feature of Third-Style wall-paintings. *Opus sectile* was made of coloured marble shapes cut to size and from different colours to create patterns that complemented the extravagant designs of Fourth-Style wall-painting.

The most extravagant and expensive mosaic known from any of the cities is that despicting the battle between Alexander the Great and Darius III of Persia in the late fourth century BC. Installed in the House of the Faun (VI.12.2), the Alexander mosaic covers around 20 square metres and must have been tortuously difficult to lay. Almost certainly copied

4.2. Pompeii: House of the Faun (VI.12.2), the Alexander mosaic (detail).
This is probably the most important piece of household decorative art found at
Pompeii, and depicts a battle between Alexander the Great and Darius of
Persia. Probably based on a now-lost Greek painting and laid in an *exedra*
between the two *peristylia*.

from a long-lost painting, it was a prestige piece of decoration in what
was the most lavishly decorated house in Pompeii – though its present
state scarcely hints at what this house once was. Its function, like so much
of the decoration in the principal rooms of a Roman house, was to serve
as a talking point that not only illustrated the wealth of the owner, but also
his tastes and interests (Fig. 4.2).

Herculaneum: the Samnite House (V.1-2)
The Samnite House lies on a corner of a crossroads in the middle of the
exposed area of Herculaneum. It occupies an area approximately equal to
6% of the the House of the Faun, one of Pompeii's largest houses, and
retains some of its early First-Style decoration in the *fauces*. Its other
interesting feature is the remarkable evidence it preserves of changes in
the use of space over several centuries.

   The Samnite House was originally built at the end of the third century
BC and covered a considerably larger area than it does now at the western
end of Insula V. By the late second or early first century BC the garden
and peristyle had been sold and the entrance to the peristyle through the
tablinum had been blocked off. The *atrium* was raised in height by adding

4.3. Herculaneum: the Samnite House, looking west. Built in the very late third century BC this house underwent a number of major alterations that reduced its accommodation but retained the massive *atrium*.

a second-storey loggia around the north and west sides (Fig. 4.3). People in the upper storey were able to look down on the *atrium* floor through the gaps between columns supporting the new ceiling. A blind colonnade of half columns was added on the south side to complete the effect. The First-Style decoration (with its characteristic use of plain coloured false-marble panels on the walls) was renewed with some Second-Style scenes.

Probably after the earthquake of AD 62 the house was reduced in size further. The gaps between the upper-storey columns were filled in so that the loggia could be used as a rental apartment, and a staircase was cut in to the north side to allow access. The First-Style decoration in the *atrium* was painted over with Fourth-Style designs. Today the First Style survives only in the *fauces*. We have no idea why the house was so drastically modified. If the early first-century BC owner was in severe financial straits it makes no sense that he sold the peristyle off only to invest in costly and complex work to create the loggia. The creation of an upstairs apartment left the house with a barn-like *atrium* that was totally disproportionate to the available living space. This recalls the vast detached Victorian houses that still stand in parts of London and provincial cities. Built for affluent families with a desire to impress and domestic servants to accommodate, these houses are anachronisms in the twenty-first century. Many have been converted into multiple apartments, leaving an incongruously large and irrelevant Victorian entrance hall which cannot be easily adapted. By 79 the Samnite House's *atrium* was probably little more than a similarly capacious relic which, had it not been for the eruption, would surely have been demolished eventually and replaced with a building more suitable for housing larger numbers of people.

Meanwhile, the House of the Grand Portal was built on the site of the Samnite House's peristyle, reusing some of its columns as fill, and these are still visible today protruding from the walls. This new house was cramped and there was not enough room even for a proper *atrium*. In compensation it had a very ornate entrance and good wall-paintings. Together the two houses provide an excellent example of the changes in living space in Pompeii and Herculaneum.

Pompeii: the House of the Menander (I.10.4)

The House of the Menander occupies most of an *insula* in the southern part of the town, fairly close to the main central crossroads. Unlike most of the other houses it has been subjected to a major modern investigation to trace its development. The House of the Menander is exceptionally large for a Pompeian house, and is one of the most luxurious. The owner was able to afford a major programme of renovation and restoration which was under way in AD 79.

The name of that original owner is unknown, though a seal belonging to Quintus Poppaeus Eros, a freedman of Quintus Poppaeus, was found in Room 43. Clearly this proves nothing since Eros might have been visiting. However, a Quintus Poppaeus served as an *aedile* in Pompeii (CC E37) and the house is so lavish and large that even if it did not belong to Quintus Poppaeus it certainly belonged to a man of his rank.

The plan of the house is asymmetrical, thanks to both the irregular dimensions of the *insula* and the house's development (Fig. 4.4). This is particularly noticeable with the placing of the peristyle off-centre to the main axis running through the *fauces* and the *atrium* (Fig. 1.4). In spite of this the visual axis was maintained by placing a symmetrical group of *exedrae* in the far (south) wall of the peristyle (nos 22-24 on the plan), but slightly to the west, so that anyone walking into the house faced directly towards them through the *atrium*, *tablinum* (no. 8) and peristyle. The axis was designed to impress the visitor with the scale of the house, enhanced by narrowing the gaps between the columns on the far (south) side of the peristyle, providing an optical illusion of exaggerated perspective: this

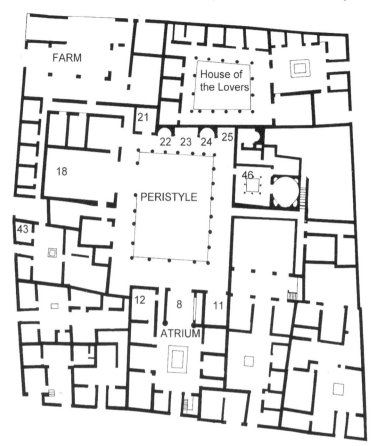

4.4. Pompeii: House of the Menander (I.10.4). Note that north is at the bottom. See text for references to the room numbers.

made the peristyle seem bigger (there are five columns on the north side, and seven on the south). The layout also distracted attention from the asymmetrical nature of the plan, and focused the visitor's attention on the literary paintings in Room 23.

Another axis was created for those dining in the large *triclinium* (dining room) (no. 18). The sequence of columns was broken and a widely-spaced pair of columns used so that those in the *triclinium* could have an unbroken view across the garden. The house's design and decoration also considered the needs of people looking out from the various rooms and niches arranged around the peristyle. Thus, rooms 12 and 21 face each other through the peristyle, and room 11 and *exedra* 25 face each other down the ambulatory on the west side of the peristyle. *Exedra* 25 may have been the shrine to the owner's ancestors.

Like many of Pompeii's major houses, this one had begun life by the late third century BC. At this time the *atrium* and its surrounding suite of rooms were in existence though it may have extended further south into the *insula*. Over the next two centuries the house grew and by the end of the first century BC it had its western bath suite, and the large asymmetrical peristyle. Between AD 50 and 62 the large *triclinium* (18) had been added, and suitable adjustments made to the columns to achieve the desired visual effect across the peristyle. Other major rooms had been added on either side and service rooms had been built behind.

Among the most important surviving painted rooms is *exedra* 23. One side of the room has the painting of the Greek Athenian comic playwright Menander, after which the house is named. There was a painting of a playwright who wrote tragedies on the other side, probably Euripides, but this is now damaged. In between, on the main rear wall was another figure, now lost. This is thought to have been Dionysus, god of the theatre, and this is the figure a visitor would have seen as he entered the house and looked down the main visual axis. The purpose was to advertise to any visitor that the owner of the House of the Menander was cultivated (or at least wished to appear so), a man of taste and style who deserved to be at the top of Pompeii's social and official ladder. Other rooms in the suite surrounding the *atrium* reinforced these pretensions with depictions of scenes connected with the Fall of Troy, and other mythical scenes. Paintings in the baths were a mixture of the aquatic and comic and are mostly Second-Style. But some are in the Fourth Style and belong to the extensive renovations and improvements of the house's last years. However, the owner retained some of the much older mosaics. Rare anywhere in Pompeii, mosaics were absent from all the other houses in the Menander's *insula* and are a further mark of the house's status.

In cellars beneath room 46 (a vestibule) in the bath suite on the west side of the house were found the remains of a wooden strongbox containing 118 pieces of decorative and valuable silver plate, vessels, and utensils, together with jewellery and coins. The silver vessels had been dismantled and carefully packed. The treasure may have been readied for removal during the events of the eruption before events overtook the owners (a number of skeletons were found in the house), or it may have been packed there for safekeeping during household repairs. According to Pliny the Elder who wrote in the last 10-15 years before the eruption, decorative silver was highly sought-after, especially if it had been manufactured by celebrated silversmiths: 'it is remarkable that gold-working has failed to make a celebrity of anyone whereas celebrated silversmiths are numerous' (*Natural History* xxx.154). Possession of such silver was a badge of rank. Showing it off proved the point.

Despite the house's evident status, one of the rooms immediately to the west of the main entrance of the house has been identified as a bar. In Pompeii high-status living sat cheek-by-jowl with the seamier side of life. It did not, apparently, trouble the wealthy Pompeians; indeed, the owner of the House of the Menander may well have owned the bar.

Pompeii: the House of Aulus Umbricius Scaurus (VII.16.15)

The family of Aulus Umbricius Scaurus the elder monopolized the Pompeii fish sauce (*garum*) trade in the mid-first century AD, using several of their freedmen to operate the concern which involved several production locations in the area. A number of inscribed containers have been

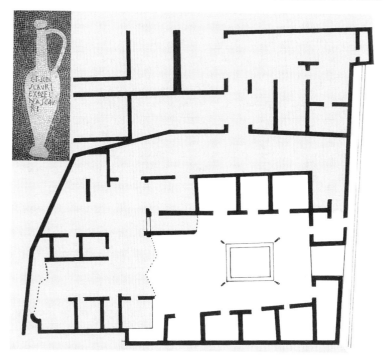

4.5. Pompeii: House of Aulus Umbricius Scaurus (VII.16.15). Built on two levels at the extreme west of town overlooking the sea, this was home to the fish-sauce manufacturer who promoted his business on mosaic panels (inset). The white area indicates the upper level with atrium. The remainder of the upper level has collapsed into the lower level (grey area).

found in and around Pompeii, testifying to the business's success. Many begin with the abbreviation GF for *garum flos*, 'prime [or flower of] fish sauce', and occasionally adding *optimum*, 'the best'.

There is no doubt about where Umbricius Scaurus lived. His house lies on the west side of Pompeii in a prestigious location that overlooked the coast in antiquity, and was only a few yards from the important temples of Venus and Apollo, the basilica and the forum (Fig. 4.5). It was built on two levels which have now partially collapsed, leaving the structure dangerous and closed to visitors. Like any important man's home, the house of Umbricius Scaurus was as much a public place as it was private. The *atrium* had a mosaic depicting miniature fish-sauce amphorae known as *urcei* and their inscriptions with the same business slogans as his real containers (CC H20ff.). Even his name may have been part of the promotion, and linked him directly with his trade. Scaurus was a common enough name, but the similar word *scarus* refers to the wrasse, a kind of fish which the Romans cultivated and caught in huge quantities off Campania (Pliny the Elder, *Natural History* ix.62). Of course this may be pure coincidence, but it is hard to see how Scaurus could have failed to notice the humorous association of his name and his trade, which can only have helped remind people what his business was.

People visiting Umbricius Scaurus to pay their respects or seek favours did so in an environment designed to reinforce their patron's status as a successful businessman. It showed that Scaurus was a man worth knowing and dealing with, and their status was enhanced through association with him. No wonder then that the council recognized the importance of honouring Scaurus the younger, magistrate, on the occasion of his premature death (see Chapter 3 and Fig. 5.2).

Pompeii: the House of Loreius Tiburtinus/Octavius Quartio (II.2.2)

This house is in complete contrast to the House of the Menander. It occupies proportionately more of an *insula* but the living space is far smaller (Fig. 4.6), and it also shares half the street frontage with another house. The house lies in the eastern part of Pompeii, with an entrance on the main east-west road through the town, and backs on to the large *palaestra* beside the amphitheatre. The house is regarded today as the prime example of a miniature version of a country villa estate transplanted to a town.

A visitor arrived at a recessed entrance door between two shops in the busy east-west road through Pompeii now known as the *Via dell'Abbondanza*. Stairways inside the house led upstairs to two open upper-story rooms above the shops. On either side of the door was a seat for waiting

4.6. Pompeii: House of Octavius Quartio (II.2.2), the main visual axis down the north-south canal that bisects the garden.

clients. In the 'standard' Roman townhouse the visitor enters the *fauces* (entrance corridor) and sees a view directly through the *atrium* and *tablinum*, and on to the peristyle, establishing the main visual axis. In this house there is no *tablinum* and the rooms around the *atrium* seem to have been of little importance. Instead the visitor reaches a small three-sided portico surrounding a very small garden, facing out on to the main garden which occupies around two-thirds of the whole *insula*. This was the most important part of the house, where the most elaborately decorated rooms were situated.

On the east side of the portico was the single most important room in the house, the *triclinium*. Since the house occupied the north-west corner of the *insula*, the dining room was located at the house's south-east corner so that it could be as close as possible to the central axis of the *insula* and the axial view of the garden. It was reached through an entrance from the portico but only once diners were inside could they appreciate the real purpose of the room. Another, wider, opening faced the south and the garden. Two canals had been used to mark out the space. The shorter east-west canal and its accompanying pergola defined where the garden began. Another, 50-metre-long, canal bisected the whole garden running its entire length on an axis centred on the *triclinium*. Diners were able to look down through the entrance towards a pavilion shrine dedicated to Diana and Actaeon and on down the large canal to the far end of the garden. The idea was to create a peaceful and pleasing view that made the garden look as impressive as possible. Unlike the House of the Menander, the vista through the atrium was of relatively little importance. In this building all the emphasis had been placed on the garden.

To entertain and impress his guests the owner had the *triclinium* painted with two friezes, one above the other. The upper frieze depicted scenes from the life of Hercules, including the moment when he made Priam king of Troy, while the lower showed episodes from the Trojan War described in the *Iliad*. Such paintings were intended to act as conversation pieces, and demonstrate the owner's tastes and interests to his visitors, appropriate to a man of refined tastes. To reinforce this, the entrance from the portico lay on another visual axis across the portico to a decorated chamber that depicted paintings of Diana and a priest of Isis. The room was evidently designed as a summer dining room. At any rate Vitruvius pointed out (vii.4.4) that soot from lamps invariably ruined dining rooms in winter, making 'paintings on grand subjects' utterly pointless.

The name of the owner is not known for certain. Painted slogans on the street frontage on both sides contribute the names Loreius and Tiburtinus, but never together. A ring found in one of the shops at the front provides Octavius Quartio. The priest of Isis is labelled as Amulius Faventinus Tiburs, who might have been the owner. Whoever owned it, this house apes the great country villas owned by the fabulously wealthy. These estates had vast gardens decorated with temples and grottoes, water features and pleasant walkways. This house seems to be an example of an attempt, perhaps by a wealthy freedman, to imitate the country homes of the upper class to which he would never be able to belong, just like Trimalchio in the *Satyricon*. Whether this owner did so with a sense of comic irony, or in all seriousness, we cannot know. The house has been described as an 'idiosyncratic and ultimately delightful petit bourgeois Disneyland' (Clarke, 207).

Herculaneum: the House of the Stags (IV.21)

The House of the Stags, named after a pair of marble statues of stags being attacked by hounds, lies at the extreme west of Herculaneum and once overlooked the seashore below. It has a very unusual lay-out designed to exploit its setting to the full (Fig. 4.7).

Entrance is through a modest side door that led into the *fauces* (A) with a marble pavement. This led to a small covered *atrium* (B) with no *impluvium* or *compluvium*, or even an axial view across it. In this house, the *atrium* was considered of little importance. The impact lay elsewhere. Here a visitor could carry straight on to a *triclinium* or *oecus* (C), turn left and be stunned by the view right down through the garden (E) to the great

4.7. Herculaneum: House of the Stags, plan (IV.21). This house's extremely unusual plan was built round its garden and central visual axis. For details, see text.

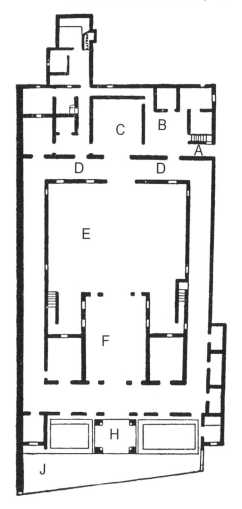

dining room at F with its completely open east and west walls and beyond through the pergola (H) to view the sea beyond. Alternatively, he could turn left and walk round the *cryptoporticus* (D) and reach the pergola that way. There was no peristyle. Everyday service rooms and accommodation were tucked away to the rear of the house.

Once at the pergola it was possible to exit the house and enjoy the sun terrace (J). Anyone viewing the garden from the *oecus* (C) looked down a central garden lined with symmetrically placed pairs of statues (Hercules and a Satyr, and the two Stags) and features (two marble tables). The great dining room (F) was virtually destroyed by early tunnellers exploring the

4.8. Herculaneum: House of the Stags (IV.21), principal view restored.

ruins. This, together with the presence of the vast lava build-up beyond the building, makes it hard to appreciate the visual impact of seeing the sea through the pergola in antiquity (Fig. 4.8).

Flooring styles marked out the status of the rooms. The *fauces* (A) had a simple tessellated floor. The most important rooms had *opus sectile* pavements. Extensive Fourth-Style paintings covered the walls of the principal rooms. The owner of the house is unknown but what really matters is the dramatic abandonment of the inward-looking convention in favour of an imaginative and pragmatic response to the setting. Visitors to this house can barely have glanced at the dingy *atrium* before being presented with the main event: a private view of the glory of the Bay of Naples framed by the house's architecture.

Herculaneum: the House in Opus Craticium (III.14)

The earthquake of AD 62 probably destroyed the original small *atrium* house on this site, and its remains were cleared away. A cheap new house was built using a wooden framework, with wattle-and-daub and plaster (*opus craticium*). By abandoning the old *atrium* design the builder of the new house could create far more living accommodation by making more efficient use of the volume available. Two apartments (on two levels) and a shop were built. By using an overhanging balcony the upper-storey space could be increased further (see Fig. 1.6). This was economically achieved with *opus craticium* even though the risk was that it was more prone to collapse and was very susceptible to fire. The result was very cramped, dark and poorly-ventilated living space. To make the new apartments attractive they were decorated with good-quality Fourth-Style paintings.

The use of *opus craticium* at this house made the most of the circum-stances created by the earthquake, and provides a very rare instance where this type of structure has survived. It was built at the same time as other home owners were renting out rooms and self-contained apartments partitioned off from existing houses. It met a need which would be much more satisfactorily mct at Ostia and Rome by the new apartment blocks. It is likely that at least two and possibly more families lived here in the last days of Herculaneum. There is also evidence from the edge of the excavated area at Herculaneum that other buildings with several storeys were being introduced.

Renting out rooms
In Pompeii's latter years there is unequivocal epigraphic evidence for property owners using their property as a source of rental income. Some may even have been acting as property developers and buying up existing buildings with a view to building up their income. A painted inscription (CC H50) records that Gnaeus Alleius Nigidius Maius owned the *insula* known to us as Region VI, Insula 6, and in antiquity as the *Insula Arriana Polliana*. Advertisements were painted up to promote the available ac-commodation which included at least one house (sometimes called the House of Pansa, VI.6.1, but now identified as Nigidius Maius' house), shops (*tabernae*) and upstairs rooms (*cenacula*). Naturally a man of Nigidius Maius' standing had nothing to do with the negotiations and tenancy agreements. Would-be tenants were directed to contact his slave Primus. This was a very convenient way for the rich to use their capital to maintain a profitable flow of cash both to service their own elite lifestyles and also their donations to civic life which they were obliged to make as the price of public office.

Ostia: the House of Apuleius (II.8.5)
The 'House of Apuleius' at Ostia was originally built in the early second century AD but went through a number of building periods, including the mid-second century, fifty or more years after the destruction of Pompeii and Herculaneum. It illustrates aspects of development not seen in those two cities. Stamps on lead water-pipes indicate that the owner of the mid-second-century AD house was Lucius Apuleius Marcellus. There is a possibility that an earlier house, built in the first century BC stood on the site, with a few fragments of *opus reticulatum* surviving.

The plan of the house initially suggests that its original lay-out resem-bled the design of Pompeian houses. The entrance led through the *fauces* into what looks like the *atrium*. However, this is no ordinary *atrium* – the

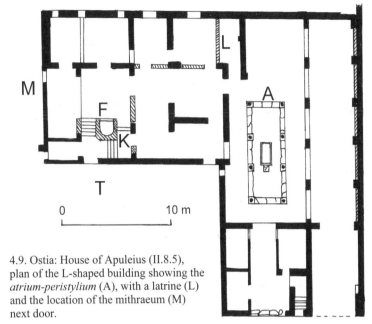

4.9. Ostia: House of Apuleius (II.8.5), plan of the L-shaped building showing the *atrium-peristylium* (A), with a latrine (L) and the location of the mithraeum (M) next door.

open area is far bigger proportionally than the *impluvia* in Pompeian houses and was surrounded by eight columns. Instead this is more like a small peristyle. A small tank in the middle channelled rainwater into the sewage system. The area seems to have been a combined *atrium* and *peristylium*, which was a matter of either choice or simply circumstance given the space available (Fig. 4.9). The house was not large but the feature managed to create an imposing sense of grandeur out of very little. The extreme rectangular proportions of the peristyle created an illusion of depth when in fact the area was extremely narrow.

The *tablinum* lay beyond this miniature atrium-peristyle but the L-shaped plot the house was built on forced a complete change of direction and the remainder of the rooms involved a right-angled turn left to the west. Here the two principal rooms were decorated with black-and-white mosaics of at least two periods, and there were other ancillary rooms, such as the kitchen. The far western part of the house was a Temple of Mithras, though it is not clear if the owner of the House of Apuleius operated the establishment.

Ostia: the Garden Houses (III.9)

It was the new harbours, first of Claudius and then of Trajan, that led to an increase in trade and population at Ostia. This forced a revolution in housing, based on new high-rise designs at Rome of which few traces survive. In the early second century AD a part of Ostia away from the busy commercial centre saw a remarkable piece of prestige property development that showed how the market for housing was changing. The development, now known as 'the Garden Houses', involved apartment blocks and shops. The date of construction of the Garden Houses can be established fairly accurately. Brick stamps have been found from the years 123-125. The oldest wall paintings and (geometric black-and-white) mosaics have been dated to 130-140.

The development must have represented a substantial investment by those who expected a good return. It was built when density of occupation was increasing, but in this case the investors were expecting to tap into a pool of more affluent potential tenants. Today we might imagine them being advertised as 'luxury apartments for rent'. Doubtless, like Julia Felix at Pompeii, the Garden Houses landlords probably promoted the flats as places suitable only for persons of suitably respectable social status. However, unlike the local worthies and pretentious freedmen of Pompeii, these would-be tenants were being offered apartments that involved living side-by-side with, above and below other families.

Although the Garden Houses *insula* was externally irregular in shape, a symmetrical internal rectangular open court was created by adjusting the width and shape of the buildings (which included the House of the Dioscures) that defined the *insula*. Within this court two identical rectangular buildings, each consisting of four identical apartments on the ground floor, were built. Doorways allowed access between some of the apartments. The buildings may have had four storeys, which would mean 32 apartments and an overall height of around 18 metres (Fig. 4.10). Evidence of lime-scale in channels leading up the walls shows that the upper floors of these apartments were supplied with water. The perimeter buildings had no equivalent facilities and their occupants must have used the basins in the open court.

A large ornamental gateway on the eastern side marked the entrance to the inner court and discouraged (or prevented) the passage of casual passers-by. The apartments were relatively large and well-appointed with good quality mosaics and paintings. The result was an exclusive development of apartments that was insulated from the bustle of Ostia's streets by the outer houses and shops.

Although a number of modifications were made over the following years, it was not until a late third-century earthquake and associated fire caused considerable damage that major changes were made. Upper floors had fallen and were not replaced. The rubble was consolidated to make a

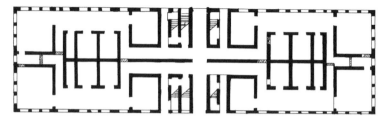

4.10. Ostia: the Garden Houses, plan of one of the two four-apartment blocks

new ground level and the buildings repaired. Most seem to have only two floors now.

The House of the Dioscures was built originally in the second century AD as part of the Garden House apartment complex where it formed the south-east corner of this development. Additions and alterations in the fourth century followed an earthquake in the late third century, when it was transformed into one of Ostia's most impressive houses, and the only one to have its own baths. In other instances, the owners of even the most well-appointed houses seem to have been satisfied with relying on public baths.

To create a sense of privacy in the fourth-century house, external windows overlooking the Garden Houses and the central court were blocked up and an external wall built to enclose the house round the east and south side. A number of internal walls were demolished to create larger rooms, and the bath suite. The contrast in the house's layout with those of the much earlier buildings at Pompeii and Herculaneum is very striking. There is far less concern with symmetry or any kind of impressive visual axes.

The Garden House complex is similar to a nearby, but much simpler, housing estate known as the *Casette-tipo*, or 'little house-type' (III.12 & 13.1-2). Built under Trajan, this also consisted of two almost identical buildings, in this case divided into two separate apartments that were mirror reflections of one another. A central wooden staircase separated the two apartments and led up to presumably at least one more pair of apartments. The buildings appear to have been more casually and cheaply built, with little concern either for accurate wall alignment or strength. This is in marked contrast to the extravagant remains of the nearby apartment block in the Insula of Serapis with its vaults and complex arched construction which still stands to a considerable height (p. 118). Unlike the Garden Houses the *Casette-tipo* development had no surrounding gardens or outer buildings to act as insulation from the rest of the town. Each apartment had its own latrine and kitchen, and decorations included monochrome mosaics and some paintings, but only traces survive. These simple apartment blocks were presumably lived in by people at the lower end of the social scale in the apartment market, especially those living in the flimsy upper storey.

Ostia: the House of Diana (III.3.3-4)

The 'House of Diana' is an extremely well-preserved apartment block in Ostia, located on the south-west corner of an *insula* and far more typical of the high-density housing being built than the Garden Houses. It survives to the height of the first-floor off-set, a protruding feature rather like a very thin balcony (Fig. 4.11). The original height is unknown, but such buildings were limited by law to 60 Roman feet (17.8 metres), sufficient for at least four stories (the approximate height of a storey was 3.5 metres), and possibly a smaller fifth. Scattered traces of similar buildings have been found in Rome, but it is Ostia which preserves this new form of Roman urban accommodation, anticipated by the creation of self-contained apartments in the older houses at Pompeii and Herculaneum, and the latter's innovative House in Opus Craticium.

The House of Diana was built in the mid-second century AD though it may have replaced an earlier version of Hadrianic date (AD 117-138). About 225-250 the floors were raised by 60 centimetres, reinforcing masonry added, and new mosaics laid – the house may therefore have suffered a partial collapse, perhaps from fire.

Unlike a Pompeian house, the upper storeys are fully integrated parts of the design, not modifications. Integral staircases entered from the street provided access to the upper floors. The rooms were generally lit from

4.11. Ostia: the House of Diana. This view of the apartment block shows the surviving remains up to the first floor.

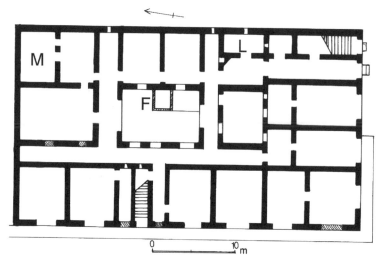

4.12. Ostia: plan of the House of Diana.

outside, rather than from the Pompeian house's internal courtyards, making another crucial difference from traditional townhouse building. This was not necessarily a good thing, especially in winter. Martial complained that the window in his Rome flat did not close properly, making the place an ice-box (*Epigrams* viii.14.5).The architect had light available only round the south and west sides (it backs on to other buildings on the north and east sides). He incorporated a small open inner court to provide light for the east and north wings. This is as small as it could be without being useless, showing that he had to provide the largest possible amount of living space.

The house is now named after a terracotta relief of Diana on the courtyard wall. No attempt was made to cover the brickwork with decoration. However, inside a number of the rooms have mosaic floors and wall-paintings dating to the time of construction and also to the early third century. Water could not be easily supplied to the upper floors so tenants made do with street fountains, though the House of Diana had its own in the central courtyard (F). A latrine was provided in the south-east corner (L). Two rooms were later converted to a mithraeum by the late second century or possibly later in the third century.

It has been suggested, on the evidence of structural anomalies and the finds of inscriptions mentioning a guild, that the ground floor of the House of Diana was used as a cult headquarters for a crossroads shrine immediately across the road, but this is unproven. In any case this will not have affected the prime function of the building, which was to accommodate a large number of people. There is some similarity here to the complex of buildings centred on the Insula of Serapis (III.10.3). Built under Hadrian, the ground floor had shops gathered round a courtyard together with a shrine to Serapis added in the early third century. A substantial brick staircase led to the upper floors and the apartments, while next door was a bath-house, reached through the Insula of Serapis. Clearly this was more than just an apartment block and served multiple functions for the immediate community (see p. 118).

*

Only a very few of the houses and apartments at Pompeii, Herculaneum and Ostia have been touched on here, but they illustrate themes that ought to be familiar to anyone with an interest in how domestic architecture has been used as an expression and consequence of status throughout the ages. Their particular value is that, unlike so many other periods and places, there is so much evidence for the use of housing at every level of the market. Like modern urban cultures, all three cities attracted growing populations that increased pressure on the available housing stock providing different opportunities for making money, whether that involved renting out street frontages, upstairs apartments, or investing in apartment block developments. Herculaneum's monumental extra-mural Villa of the Papyri is beyond the scope of this book but it exemplifies the super-rich culture that so many of the homeowners of Pompeii and Herculaneum tried to emulate with varying degrees of success, depending on their tastes, aspirations, limitations and circumstances.

Chapter 5

Status and Prestige in Death

A number of tombs have already been mentioned in this book, for the funerary monuments of Pompeii and Ostia are among the most important records these towns have produced (apart from the tomb of Marcus Nonius Balbus, very little is known about Herculaneum's cemeteries). They tell us about the population, sometimes in their own words, and in the most valuable cases they provide detailed biographical information, a vital tool for understanding who these people were, what they did, and what status they either held or felt they ought to hold, in their communities.

The Pompeian cemeteries

By law, Roman cemeteries were built outside the settled area. Burials within a town, such as that of Marcus Nonius Balbus at Herculaneum, required exceptional circumstances. The best existing surviving examples anywhere are outside the Herculaneum and Nuceria Gates at Pompeii (Fig. 5.1). Like the houses and public buildings within Pompeii, they advertised a person's status by announcing his or her achievements in life both through the explicit records of acts, honours or funeral costs and implicitly in the quality of the tomb. The Nuceria Gate cemetery is monopolized by the graves of successful freedmen and their families. The Herculaneum Gate cemetery is more mixed, with graves of prominent members of the decurial class nearer to the gate. Whatever their status, the deceased remained a member of the family. Here his or her descendants, and clients and freedmen, came to pay their respects. The more esteemed the deceased person, the more esteemed these people were by association. Coming to the tomb and taking part in an annual commemoration showed they were worthy of respect too, and might well expect to be buried there themselves. It was also a public affirmation of their status.

The tombs of Mamia and Marcus Porcius

The scattering of modest graves around the more elaborate ones in Pompeii's cemeteries creates a sense of haphazard cemetery development. This, however, was not the case. Persons of high status were eligible for civic honours in the form of a cash gratuity to pay for the funeral, the

5.1. Pompeii: street of tombs outside the Herculaneum Gate. Far left: tomb of Aulus Umbricius Scaurus the younger, centre: tomb of Gaius Calventius Quietus, right: tomb of Naevoleia Tyche.

tomb itself and a prestige location close to the city gate. The most important individuals received all three benefits. The most prestigious tombs were designed as large semi-circular stone benches with seat ends carved in the form of a lion's leg, and with other features such as altars. Known as *exedra* (or *schola*) seat-tombs, two of these lie close to the Herculaneum Gate. One was dedicated to Aulus Veius who had served as a Pompeian *duumvir* twice and as a *quinquennalis* (CC G4). Nearby the other is the tomb of Mamia, a public priestess (CC E40). She had paid for a temple in Pompeii's forum (possibly the one now known as the Temple of Vespasian, or more accurately the Imperial Cult), in the forum next to Eumachia's building.

In between was the altar tomb of Marcus Porcius (CC B12). Marcus Porcius appears to have been one of the original colonists installed in Pompeii in 80 BC by Publius Cornelius Sulla in the aftermath of the Social War. He served as a *duumvir*. Inscriptions record him in this capacity taking part in organizing key activities very soon after this date. He was involved in issuing contracts for the dedication of an altar in the Temple of Apollo, and the building of the Odeon or 'covered theatre'. Along with his fellow *duumvir* Gaius Quinctius Valgus he paid for the amphitheatre out of his own pocket. No wonder then that the council voted a site for his tomb in one of the most prominent locations available.

The tombs of Gaius Vestorius Priscus and Marcus Obellius Firmus
Two thousand sesterces seems to have been a fairly standard funeral grant voted by the town council of Pompeii. It was a significant sum of money, but a trifle compared to what a magistrate was expected to spend on the town from his own resources while in office and the property qualification needed to get there (see Chapter 2, p. 26). Gaius Vestorius Priscus had become an *aedile* by the age of 22. He had had little time to make his mark on Pompeii when he died, but the council voted the usual 2000 sesterces for his funeral, while his grieving mother Mulvia Prisca paid for the tomb and its wall-paintings depicting a silver service and gladiatorial games which still stands outside the Vesuvian Gate (see Fig. 2.2; CC F88).

Two thousand sesterces was also awarded to Aulus Umbricius Scaurus the elder to pay for his son's funeral, the difference being that Scaurus the younger had progressed some way in his career and had become a *duumvir* (Fig. 5.2). However, Marcus Obellius Firmus, *aedile* and *duumvir*, was not only awarded 5,000 sesterces for his funeral but also received a number of other gifts from Pompeii's suburban country district (CC G12). Oddly though, his tomb outside the Nola Gate is rather less imposing than that of Vestorius Priscus. Perhaps Priscus' mother had a higher opinion of her son's achievements (or at least his potential) than the Pompeian councillors.

5.2. Pompeii: the tomb of Aulus Umbricius Scaurus the younger, recording his duumvirate, the donation by the council of 2,000 sesterces for his funeral, and an equestrian statue, and that his father erected the tomb.

5.3. Pompeii: tombs outside the Nuceria Gate. Left to right: tomb of Publius Flavius Philoxenus and Flavia Agathea, unknown tomb, tomb of Eumachia, tomb of Marcus Octavius and Vertia Philumena

The tomb of Eumachia

Eumachia's conspicuous building by Pompeii's forum has already been discussed in some detail (Chapter 3). Despite this, and her role as a public priestess, curiously she was not voted the honour of a public *exedra* seat tomb like the one awarded Mamia, though this may be connected with the practice becoming obsolete by the time she died. Eumachia's tomb, the largest found at Pompeii, is a semi-circular *exedra* almost 14 metres wide and over 13 metres deep, decorated with a frieze of Amazons. It was set back from the road and access was only through a gate in a wall that fronted the massive tomb (Fig. 5.3). The inscriptions merely state that it was built by Eumachia for herself and her family (CC E47). No other individuals are mentioned, and no mention is made of her lifetime achievements.

The main curiosity about Eumachia's tomb is its location and who used it. It is incongruously located in the Nuceria Gate cemetery which is otherwise dominated by the tombs of freedmen. Presumably Eumachia and her son were buried there, but the only actual person stated to have been interred was a 20-year-old man called Lucius Eumachius Aprilis, probably a freedman of Eumachia (CC G16). By the mid-first century AD it was being used by the family of Gnaeus Alleius Nigidius Maius (including his mother, Pomponia Decharcis), celebrated as Pompeii's greatest giver of gladiatorial games (CC G17). Eumachia and her son Marcus Numistrius Fronto have left no trace of descendants so it is possible that the Alleii, into which Nigidius Maius had been adopted, were connected with Eumachia in some way and perhaps had inherited her estate. It is also possible they had simply bought the tomb or space in it, something which certainly happened at Ostia (see below).

Naevoleia Tyche

Freedmen, although excluded from public office, had other opportunities to become prominent members of their communities. Naturally, they expected appropriate acknowledgement. If it was not, then steps might have to be taken. Gaius Munatius Faustus was a freedman, married to a freedwoman called Naevoleia Tyche. They lived in the suburban country district outside Pompeii, and by the reign of Nero (AD 54-68) he had done well. In fact *faustus* means 'fortunate' or 'prosperous' though this may merely have been an optimistic name given him when he was born. Once freed, he rose to become an *Augustalis*, a priest of the imperial cult. He prepared himself a tomb in Pompeii's Nuceria Gate cemetery with this inscription (CC G38):

> G.MVNATIVS.FAUSTVS
> AVGVSTAL.ET.PAGAN.DD.SIBI.ET
> NAEVOLEIAE.TYCHI.CONIVGI

> Gaius Munatius Faustus, Augustalis and Country Dweller by decree
> of the councillors, for himself and his wife Naevoleia Tyche

This tomb also featured inscriptions which record how members of his household were buried there too. They include several small children, slaves and freedmen. It was a monument to the status he had achieved in Pompeii's broader community, but it is interesting that his position as a freedman is unstated and is implied only through his role as an *Augustalis*.

The second tomb only commemorates Munatius Faustus since he was never buried in it, though it seems his wife and other members of the household were. An altar tomb, it was erected outside the Herculaneum Gate by his widow to commemorate the honours her husband had received, which had included the honorific double chair (*bisellium*) in the theatre or amphitheatre (see Fig. 5.1). It was an expensive monument that sits on a large plinth so as to be as conspicuous as possible to passers-by. The cremations were deposited in glass urns contained within a vault beneath the altar. Unlike the first tomb, it is a good deal more brash and explicit. Naevoleia Tyche unequivocally stated that they were freedman and freedwoman. She also recorded how they had risen to the point where they had slaves of their own and had freed them too (CC G47). There is no indication that Faustus and

Naevoleia had had children. If they had done so they could have expected their freeborn sons would have been able to enter public office.

> NAEVOLEIA.L.LIB TYCHE SIBI ET
> C. MVNATIO FAVSTO AVG ET PAGANO
> CVI DECVRIONES CONSENSV POPVLI
> BISELLIVM OB MERITA EIVS DECREVERVNT
> HOC MONIMENTVM NAEVOLEIA TYCHE LIBERTIS SVIS
> LIBERTABVSQV ET C. MVNATI FAVSTI VIVA FECIT

Naevoleia Tyche, freedwoman of Lucius, for herself and Gaius Munatius Faustus, Augustalis and Country District Dweller for whom the town councillors (*decuriones*) decreed an honorific chair for his merits by consent of the people. This monument Naevoleia Tyche had made while she lived, for her own freedmen and freed-women and those of Gaius Munatius Faustus.

Naevoleia Tyche was determined that her status, acquired through her husband's achievements, be conspicuously commemorated, and no doubt she was equally unashamed of their backgrounds. That a carving of her own bust was included overlooking the inscription shows that her purpose was also to make sure her status as his wife was properly marked. But appropriately enough Tyche comes from the Greek *tyche*, 'god-given fortune', and thus means the same as her husband's cognomen. Both she and Munatius Faustus had lived up to their names; by commissioning this monument Naevoleia Tyche showed that she was in a position to pay for it. What little we know about the pair resonates in Petronius' scathing depiction of the freedman Trimalchio and his pretensions.

Gaius Calventius Quietus was another Pompeian *Augustalis*. Like Munatius Faustus he was voted a *bisellium*, which was proudly depicted on his tomb close to the one Naevoleia had erected to her husband. That he was a freedman is implied only by the fact that he was an *Augustalis* and does not appear to have held public office. The tomb is designed to be seen, and specified that he had earned this honour due to his *munificentia* ('generosity') (Fig. 2.7; CC G37).

The Ostian cemeteries
The Ostian burials lined the roads leading out of Ostia to the south-east, east towards Rome, and north towards Portus (Fig. 5.4). These cemeteries covered several miles in each direction so it is no great surprise that only certain parts of them have been investigated. The areas most examined in

5.4. Ostia: Isola Sacra, house tombs. Mostly second century AD.

detail are the tombs just outside Ostia's eastern gate on the road to Rome, the Via Ostiensis, and the Isola Sacra group of graves along the road to Portus, now a small archaeological site in the farmland just to the east of the busy main road heading to Fiumicino Airport.

Very few persons of high social status seem to have used these cemeteries, though perhaps the richest graves lay much further from the settlement. Alternatively they may have sought to be commemorated in different ways, such as by public statues. Many of the most important families, especially of imperial officials, will have been rich enough to own major private country estates and been buried there. Some of the town magistrates were buried on the Rome road but in general the cemeteries were occupied by artisans, merchants, shopkeepers, and their families. The inscriptions which survive are usually limited to statements of name, age, and family associates.

By the early first century AD a new type of tomb, the *columbarium*, had begun to appear. These tombs consisted of brick-built vaulted chambers with recesses lining the wall for cremation urns and sometimes for inhumations (used from the reign of Hadrian on) as well. They often had quite elaborate doorways in elegant decorative facades which displayed a marble inscription to identify the occupants, and who had taken care of the funeral. Within, wall-paintings featured symbols of the afterlife such as birds and appropriate scenes from myth or of the gods.

Sometimes the occupation of the deceased is illustrated on the tomb. One of the Ostian Isola Sacra tombs has a terracotta relief of a man

5.5. Ostia: Isola Sacra, terracotta reliefs from tombs depicting the owner's occupation, in these cases knives and tools, and grain shipping.

surrounded by a display of tools and sharpening a knife (Fig. 5.5 left), similar to trade signs posted outside the places of business at Pompeii. Verrius Euhelpistus and his wife Verria Zosime were clearly proud of the family trade. Their tomb defined Verrius, and it defined his family. Their visiting descendants would know who he was, and what he had been, just as Tiberius Claudius Eutychus displayed a terracotta relief showing a corn grinder on one side of his tomb entrance and on the other a relief showing a (grain?) ship (Fig. 5.5 right).

A number of these tombs survive at the Isola Sacra in a remarkable state of preservation, buried by coastal sand dunes in antiquity. Some of these tombs had outdoor dining couches immediately in front of the entrance. Here visiting family members could dine in the company of their ancestors during the *Parentalia* festival. These tombs symbolize the increasing wealth available to relatively modest members of the Ostian community. Some of the memorial slabs also made it clear how much actual grave area was owned. A freedwoman called Clodia Prepusa stated on her memorial slab that the tomb's frontage covered 'twenty feet' and sat in a 'forty-foot plot'. Another, for the family of Marcus Antonius Vitalis, included a warning that if anyone other than a family member (which included their freedmen and freedwomen) was buried there a fine would be payable. However, it is equally clear from other tombs that it was possible to sell on spare space, which might mean anything from dividing the chamber in two to nothing more than a spare wall niche for a cremation urn.

Less affluent individuals were buried in graves scattered around the richer burials. Some had simple masonry sarcophagi, but the poorest had just an amphora to contain their cremated ashes. One of the most idiosyncratic is the tomb of Gaius Annaeus Atticus whose cremated remains were buried beneath a small brick pyramid with a marble inscription recording his name (Fig. 5.6). No explanation for this curious choice of tomb was given on the inscription, though his name suggests he came from Attica in Greece. He may either have had trading connections with the Egyptian corn route or perhaps just a fancy, based either on personal experience of the pyramids or because he had been taken by the impressive and still extant 36.4-metre-high pyramid tomb of Cestius built *c.* 18-12 BC outside the Ostian gate of Rome. Atticus' tomb is little more than a metre in height, but there was nothing new about people of his status imitating the Roman elite in a very modest way.

By the mid-third century the known Ostian cemeteries seem to have fallen out of use, other than burials being inserted into existing tombs and graves. This may have been an economy measure as Ostia's importance declined, but may also simply reflect less concern about pagan burial practices in an increasingly Christian era. Once Christianity was legitimized in the fourth century under Constantine (307-337) burials were more likely to take place in and around the new churches. The old cemeteries became handy sources of spare stone. In Ostia's House of the Porch during the fourth century an old tombstone was made into a drain cover and inserted in the ambulatory around the peristyle, without any attempt being made to erase the remaining lettering and its pagan abbreviations. Whatever the attempts in life to express status and to perpetuate that afterwards, death was, as ever, the great leveller.

5.6. Ostia: Isola Sacra, pyramid tomb of Gaius Annaeus Atticus.

Chapter 6

Destruction, Excavation and Preservation

24 August AD 79

The principal accounts of the eruption of Mount Vesuvius on 24 August AD 79 during the reign of Titus (79-81) are the surviving letters of Pliny the Younger, who witnessed the event, provides the date and describes not only the epic drama of the eruption itself but also how his uncle, Pliny the Elder, then commanding the fleet at *Misenum*, died while leading a rescue expedition (*Letters* vi.16 and 20, see pp. 107-11). It has been recently suggested that the eruption may actually have occurred as late as October. The evidence for this is the discovery at Pompeii of a coin of Titus, which it is claimed cannot have been struck before September 79, and traces of plants and autumn clothing. However, it has since been revealed that the coin is too damaged to be read reliably and that other organic evidence in the form of fish sauce from the house of Umbricius Scaurus suggests a summer date based on the species of fish used.

So there is no reliable reason yet to reject Pliny's date, nor would it really make any difference to our understanding of what happened. The cities were destroyed in very different ways. Lying 10 kilometres (6 miles) from the volcano, Pompeii was bombarded by episodes of volcanic debris that rained down across the city. The bombardment lasted intermittently for around 20 hours. The pumice, lava, ash and rock filled the buildings, trapping those who had remained or were unable to leave. This was followed by a superheated surge of hot ash and gas which together finally buried the city under a carpet of rubble up to three metres deep. Anyone trying to make an escape on foot during this time would have found wading through the debris impossible, quite apart from the heat and poisonous gases pervading the atmosphere. Death was certain for those left behind.

The material hurled out by the volcano pulverized roofs and upper storeys, and offered very limited preservative conditions for organic materials, complicated by the fact that any wooden fittings, such as door and crucial load-bearing lintels, simply rotted away in the normal course of events. The removal of the volcanic overburden reveals walls and features suspended by that overburden which would promptly collapse without immediate consolidation and replacement of those key missing parts. In many instances the houses' remains were rendered even more unstable by Roman salvage parties. The tight packing of the ash and lava does sometimes mean that the void left by the decayed wood can be filled with plaster and a cast taken before removal of the volcanic fill. This has, for example, revealed the shape and design of shop shutters. The same process has also revealed the remains of the Pompeians themselves. The relatively intact houses which can be explored today are the product of laborious reconstruction.

Herculaneum was struck by superheated pyroclastic surges which covered the seven kilometres (4.2 miles) from the volcano in a terrifyingly short time and wiped out the city, while some of Pompeii's terrified inhabitants still had time to escape. This volcanic ash and mud surged down the volcano's slopes at high speed literally boiling alive any human beings and animals. It also normally turned wood into carbon, which has no structural strength, but which preserved the original form of the wooden fittings and furniture, making reconstruction and repair a more reliable process even if it is immensely more time-consuming, expensive and complex to achieve (Figs 1.6 and 6.1).

The surge buried Herculaneum to a depth of twenty-three metres or more and pushed back the coastline almost half a kilometre. It was thought

6.1. Herculaneum from the air. Centre: the House of the Wooden Partition. To its immediate left, the flat-roofed House in Opus Craticium and then the House of the Bronze Herm. Lower right: the atrium of the Samnite House. The area at the lower left shows the heavily-damaged walls of houses excavated earlier without proper consolidation.

originally that the inhabitants had had time to escape, since almost no human remains have been found within Herculaneum, but excavations in recent years on the ancient waterfront have revealed groups of skeletons gathered together in the vaulted recesses beneath the stone revetment marking the tragic ends of groups of peoples gathered together.

Imperial help was forthcoming for those who survived the disaster. Titus, who had only been emperor for a month when the eruption occurred, dispatched two proconsuls to Campania to take care of disaster relief. There was little practical assistance anyone could offer and the main contribution was to hand out money, bolstered by distributing the estates of people who had been killed and left no heirs. This was recorded by Suetonius (*Titus* 8.4) by the early second century, but also by the historian Dio, writing in the early third century. Unlike Suetonius, Dio actually specifies Herculaneum and Pompeii as the destroyed cities, showing how much long-term impact the destruction had had on Roman consciousness (lxvi.24).

Discovery and excavation

Ostia was never lost and continued to feature occasionally in medieval events. In the 1300s the custom house at Ostia was Rome's most important and the road to Rome a significant commercial artery. By the eighteenth century Ostia was beginning to attract antiquarian attention – unlike Rome it was not buried by medieval development. Excavations began in the nineteenth century, but it was really the Fascist archaeological campaigns of the late 1930s that exposed Ostia's remains. Extensive clearance and restoration of the ruins have uncovered around half of the city, and also parts of its cemeteries. Trajan's hexagonal harbour remains a prominent landmark, though Claudius' harbour is completely buried beneath the outskirts of Rome's Fiumicino airport.

Pompeii and Herculaneum were also beneficiaries of the rising interest in the ancient world. However, the first visitors to the ruins of Pompeii were not the gentlemen of the European Enlightenment but her surviving population. After the eruption the superstructure of some public buildings helped salvagers find their way around the devastated city, a tradition which lasted on into the Middle Ages (Fig. 6.2). Excavation work has shown that a number of buildings, for example the House of the Menander, were visited after the eruption by tunnellers and opportunists who tried to recover valuables and other precious possessions by digging into the ruins. In some cases the visitors, looters or the original owners, hacked their way through walls as they tried to make their way round houses. Salvage work continued into medieval times, preserving knowledge that a city lay buried there, but also resulting in removal of stonework and

6.2. Pompeii: the Temple of Jupiter and part of the forum colonnade (restored). Locating buried public buildings allowed surviving Pompeians to remove useful stone, find houses and recover valuables.

contributing to the present derelict state of the forum. Herculaneum was inaccessible to the Romans and was left untouched.

It was 1594 when workmen diverting the River Sarno crossed the site of ancient Pompeii and uncovered inscriptions and buildings. But no one at the time made the connection with the ancient references to Pompeii, even though the site had long been known as *Cività*, 'the Ancient Town'. It was not until the mid-eighteenth century that more attention was paid to the sixteenth-century discoveries, when an inscription was found in 1763 naming Pompeii and finally confirming its identity. Excavations followed, reaching their climax in the late nineteenth and early twentieth centuries.

Considering the vastly greater depths at which it lies, it is ironic that Herculaneum was first explored in the early 1700s after workmen digging a well hit the remains of the theatre. Impossible to excavate by the standards of the day, not least because of the overlying modern settlement, Herculaneum's theatre was ravaged by explorers who dug deep tunnels down through the solidified volcanic mud in search of antiquities for wealthy patrons. The work was conducted by Emmanuel Maurice de Lorraine, Prince d'Elboeuf. His men hit on an almost perfectly preserved theatre complete with all its statuary and facilities. Tragically, he ordered the recovery of every piece of statuary possible, without making any record.

In 1738 more tunnellers arrived at Herculaneum, smashing through walls as they came to them. In 1828 excavations resumed, this time with a determination to expose the remains properly. Piecemeal efforts followed in the nineteenth century but cost and logistics meant the work was very limited. It was not until the late 1920s with funding from the Fascist government that the work really expanded but to date only four *insulae* have been completely exposed. Herculaneum's upper storeys and wooden fittings have often survived, making for extremely expensive and complex consolidation work as the buildings are slowly extracted from their entombment. However, the present state of some buildings is misleading. The Samnite House today appears to be almost intact but when it was discovered in 1927 most of the upper part of its lofty *atrium* was shattered (Fig. 4.3). Today, work at Herculaneum is very limited since maintaining the structures already exposed is a crisis in its own right.

Pompeii was much more easily excavated and today around two-thirds lie exposed. Some of this work was carried out in the nineteenth century but real archaeological progress took place from the 1920s with a determination to consolidate, restore, and present houses as much as possible in their original form. Nevertheless, many of the archaeological conclusions drawn at the time from that work have been questioned in more recent times. However, nothing can alter the fact that the ability to excavate in both cities artefacts which were abandoned in their original context provides a unique opportunity to understand how Roman life functioned.

All three cities present unique archaeological problems. It is very difficult to explore the development of each building, since it would be almost impossible to justify the destructive excavation needed to seek out earlier phases. Judicious use of targeted excavation is being increasingly used where the potential damage is minimal and outweighed by the evidence recovered.

Excavation leaves ancient remains exposed to the elements and no longer protected by the accumulation of debris. Pompeii, Herculaneum and Ostia present special problems because their excavation revealed partially intact buildings. Any building, whatever its age, requires continuous maintenance. Ancient structures with crumbling mortar and concrete deteriorate more quickly. Many of the ancient houses are unroofed, letting in harsh sunlight, water, wind, animals and vegetation. Antiquarian collectors, vandalism, theft, indifference, financial issues and other problems have confounded efforts to keep more than a small proportion of the better-preserved houses open to the public.

Today conservation is a far higher priority than exposing any more buildings to add to the hundreds already excavated. There are ongoing major archaeological projects with international organizations determined to achieve a much more detailed understanding of how Pompeii and Herculaneum evolved but with a commitment to conserving the extant structures first. In 2008 the authorities announced a state of emergency and a determination to find a proper solution to repairing the damage before it is too late. Already walls and buildings have crumbled, wall-paintings have deteriorated beyond redemption, and both Pompeii and Herculaneum present visitors with numerous signs barring access across streets and house entrances.

The Herculaneum Conservation Project (HCP) was set up in 2001 to conserve and enhance the site as a joint venture between the Soprintendenza Archeologica di Pompei and the Packard Humanities Institute, with the British School at Rome. The idea is to make good the damage caused by a long period of neglect, test and execute conservation strategies, record and publish findings, and publicize the site and its study. As part of the initiative an International Centre for the Study of Herculaneum has now also been established near the site. Nevertheless, it is very important to recognize that however much money and effort is poured into conserving Pompeii and Herculaneum, the process of decay can only be slowed down, and not stopped, as HCP's long-term plan acknowledges.

Understanding and reaching the cities today

Very little is known today about how Ostians, Pompeians and Herculaneans referred to the houses, streets and areas of their cities. The system used today is modern and this should be remembered when using it. Pompeii and Ostia are divided into Regions, allocated a Roman numeral. Each Region covers several *insulae*, each of which is given its own number. Region VI in Pompeii for example covers the north-west part of the city and has sixteen *insulae*. Individual houses are normally given a name that refers to either the original Roman owners, or some other distinctive feature of the house, and a number referring to its principal entrance. Thus the House of the Menander at Pompeii is Region I, Insula 10, Entrance 4, abbreviated to I.10.4 (or I.x.4). Where a house has multiple entrances or components this is also reflected in the name. Thus the House of Umbricius Scaurus is referenced as VII.16.12-15 (or VII.xvi.12-15). Herculaneum's exposed area is too small to require division into Regions. Here buildings are simply referred to by *insula* and building number.

Reaching all three sites is easy today. Flights to Rome are easily available from Britain and at the time of writing scheduled direct flights to Naples operate from London Gatwick, and London Stansted. Ostia is best visited by taking Rome's Linea B metro to Piramide station, then walking a few yards to the adjacent Lido di Ostia station and taking the overground train out to Ostia Antica (about thirty minutes). From the station it takes about ten minutes to walk to the ruins. Rome's metro tickets are valid on both legs of the journey. The *Isola Sacra* tombs require more persistence. They lie close to the road that connects Ostia Antica with Fiumicino airport and can be located on Google Earth at 46° 14' 10" N, 12° 15' 48" E. The only way easy way to reach them is with independent coach or car transport. Public transport via the Cotral bus service from Ostia Antica is feasible but complicated by the need to have pre-purchased tickets and the one-way road system.

Pompeii and Herculaneum are easily reached by taking the Circumve-suviana line that runs between Naples and Sorrento. Both have their own stations though the walk down from Ercolano's station is a little further than that from Pompeii's. Teachers and students receive discounts on production of proof of status.

Access to many of the principal houses at Pompeii and Herculaneum is now restricted to previously-booked groups. The procedure is as follows:

- Contact should be made with the Soprintendenza Archeologica di Pompei at http://www.pompeiisites.org/ – Via Villa dei Misteri, 2 80045 Pompei (NA) – tel. (+39) 081 8575111, fax (+39) 081 8613183. The request, preferably made by fax, should specify the number of people, the specific houses or buildings for which a visit is requested, the educational purpose of the visit, and the date.
- If the visit is approved, the Soprintendenza's office will issue a permit by fax or email which will specify the buildings and the date(s), and provide telephone numbers for l'Ufficio Scavi di Pompei, and Ercolano.
- A telephone call to l'Ufficio Scavi di Pompei, or Ercolano, (as appro-priate) must then be made shortly before the actual visit(s) to arrange a specific time so that staff can be available to let the group in.
- The group leader must then present the permit at Pompeii or Hercu-laneum on arrival and confirm with site staff the time each house or building is to be visited.

It is important to be aware that even armed with a permit, a group may not be allowed access on the day if restoration work is under way or if any other conditions prevent access for safety or practical reasons. For the same reasons, it may be possible to visit only parts of the building(s) requested. Staff shortages may also prevent access on the day. Those leading educational visits would therefore be wise to be flexible and not rely too much on access to locked buildings.

Many of Pompeii and Herculaneum's best finds are in the National Archaeological Museum in Naples. This is easy to reach by metro or on foot (30 minutes) from Napoli Centrale railway station. However, it is impossible to predict which displays will be open on any given occasion.

6.3. Mosaic from a *triclinium* of a Pompeii house (I.5.2). The skull is suspended from a plumb line between symbols of wealth (left) and poverty (right), indicating prophetically that death will come to rich and poor alike. Now in Naples Museum.

Glossary

aedilis (English: *aedile*): junior magistrate (two) responsible for the maintenance of public buildings, games and services. The word is linked to *aedes*, 'temple', and *aedificare*, 'to build'.

atrium: the main hall of the *domus*, reached by the *fauces*. The main public area where guests were greeted, domestic rituals performed. Surrounded by private chambers (e.g. *cubicula*), and normally with an *impluvium* and *compluvium*,

biclinium: dining room with only two couches, e.g. in the House of Octavius Quartio. See also *triclinium*.

bisellium: the honorific 'double seat' awarded to civic worthies in the theatre and amphitheatre. Such an honour could continue posthumously.

cenaculum: originally an upstairs dining room, but came to mean an upstairs or attic room lived in by poorer people.

collegium: corporation or guild of members of the same profession. See also *schola* below.

compluvium: opening in the roof, usually in an *atrium*, allowing rain (*pluvia*) to fall down to the *impluvium*.

curia: the Senate or town council

decuriones (Eng.: decurion): town councillor. To be eligible a candidate normally had to have served as an aedile first, fulfilled the local property qualification for office, reached the age of 25, and been elected. The word means literally *de curia*, '[member] of the assembly/senate'.

duoviri, see *duumvir*.

duumvir: one of the two senior urban magistrates. A candidate had to have been an aedile first. Usually addreviated to II.VIR.

equites: members of the *ordo equester* (equestrian order), the second tier of Roman aristocracy, below the senate. Historically, an *eques* was wealthy enough to supply a horse with which to fulfil his military service. By imperial times this was obsolete, and all an *eques* had to possess was the 400,000 sesterces property qualification.

exedra: an open curved or square recess set into a wall, for example those on the south side of the peristyle in the House of the Menander. Also applied to public seat tombs such as that of Mamia.

fauces: literally 'jaws' and applied to the corridor of a house between the entrance and the *atrium*.

garum: fish sauce made from fermented fish. Extremely popular in the Roman world, and extensively exported.

impluvium: small rectangular recess or pool in the floor of the *atrium* to catch water from the *compluvium* above.

lararium: small household shrine depicting, or housing statues of, household spirits, the *lares*.

oecus: a room with a view, usually applied to a more important room, for example the *triclinium* in the House of Octavius Quartio.

opus craticium: building technique involving a timber frame filled with rubble masonry and plastered. Susceptible to fire.

opus incertum: building technique involving rubble walls held together with cement.

opus mixtum: building technique involving alternate layers of brick and stone, usually two or three layers of brick for each of stone.

opus reticulatum: building technique involving small square stones laid in diagonal lines. The corners of such walls were usually brick and tile.

opus sectile: floor work made of thin slices of ornamental stone cut into shapes and set into patterns.

ordo decurionum: the 'order of decurions', i.e. the body of men on the council.

ordo senatorius (Eng.: senatorial): the upper tier of Roman society, which required property to the value of 1 million sesterces. Men of the senatorial order were eligible to stand for a series of magistracies. Election to the junior magistracy of *quaestor* qualified the man to enter the Senate of Rome and began a career path culminating in the consulship. Such men, for example Marcus Nonius Balbus, could expect to command legions and provinces as they reached the climax of their careers.

Parentalia: religious festival held 13-21 February to commemorate deceased ancestors of the family at their tombs by celebrating a feast.

peristylium (Eng: *peristyle*): colonnaded area, for example a garden area surrounded by a colonnade within a house.

quinquennales: every five years the elected pair of *duoviri* were given special responsibilities for compiling a census of people who possessed the appropriate property qualification to serve as magistrates and on the city council.

schola: (1) a place for learned conversation, applied to the *exedra* seat tombs at Pompeii; (2) a *collegium* or guild, and the place where the guild met.

seviri Augustales: priests of the imperial cult. The order was open to freedmen, making it their most important route to status in urban communities.

tablinum: a room, usually located between the *atrium* and the *peristylium*, where the householder stored his documents and records.

triclinium: the dining room, so named because of the couches ranged on three sides of the room. In the Roman *domus*, the summer *triclinium* frequently looks out across the *peristylium*. See also *biclinium*.

tufa: porous rock made from calcium carbonate.

tuff: a porous and light rock made from volcanic deposits that has become compacted and compressed. Used by the Romans for wall blocks, columns, and roads. Latin = *tofus*, Italian = *tufo*. Sometimes confused with *tufa*.

Selected Texts and Inscriptions

This section includes some of the less easily found literary texts and inscriptions referred to in this book. Others may be found in a variety of sources such as the Penguin Classics series, the Loeb Classical Library and online at http://penelope.uchicago.edu/Thayer/E/Roman/home.html

Strabo, *Geography* v.3.5 – the city of Ostia
The coastal cities of the Latii are, first, Ostia: it has no harbour because of the silting up caused by the Tiber, which is fed by numerous streams. Now although it is at great risk that the merchant-ships anchor way out in the swell, it is the prospect of grain which takes priority. In fact it is the good supply of tenders, which offload the cargoes and bring cargoes in exchange, that makes it possible for the ships to sail away quickly before they reach the Tiber. Alternatively, after being off-loaded of part of their cargo, they sail into the Tiber and head inland as far as Rome, which is 190 stadia [equal to about 35 kilometres, about 21 miles]. Ostia was founded by Ancus Marcius. Such then is the city of Ostia.

Pliny the Elder, *Natural History* ix.14-15 – a whale at Ostia
A whale was seen in the port at Ostia fighting with the Emperor Claudius. It came at the time when Claudius was completing the harbour works, being tempted by a wrecked ship's cargo of hides imported from Gaul. In gorging itself for several days it ploughed into the shallow seabed with waves heaping sand up so high that it was not able to turn round in any manner and, while it pursued its feast (which was propelled by the waves towards the shore), its back projected way above the water like a capsized boat. Claudius ordered that many nets be stretched across the harbour's mouth, and setting out himself with the praetorian cohorts he offered a show to the Roman people with soldiers throwing spears from the ships as the whale rose up, one of which we saw sunk by being filled with water from the whale's snorting.

Pliny the Younger, *Letters* **vi.16, to Cornelius Tacitus**
You ask me to write you something about the death of my uncle, which you can leave to posterity as a reliable account. I am thankful, for I see that his death will be remembered forever if you record it.

He died in the destruction of the loveliest landscape, in a memorable disaster which affected peoples and cities alike, but this will be a form of eternal life for him. Although he wrote many long-lasting books himself, the indestructible nature of what you write will vastly add to his immortality. In my view the lucky ones are those who are born to do something worth writing about, or to write something worth reading. The luckiest, of course, are those who do both. My uncle will be counted amongst the latter for his own books and yours.

So with great pleasure I have taken up, or taken upon myself, the job you have given me. My uncle was at Misenum during his time in command of the fleet. On the 24th August at the seventh hour of daylight my mother alerted him to an unusually large cloud of strange appearance. At the time he was resting after dinner with his book, following some sunbathing and a cold bath. He had his shoes brought and then climbed up to where he could get the best view of the phenomenon. The cloud was rising from a mountain too far away to identify, but afterwards we discovered it was Vesuvius.

I can best describe it as looking like a pine tree rather than any other sort. It rose up into the sky on a very long 'trunk' from which 'branches' spread out. I suppose it had been pushed up by a sudden blast, which then lost its force, leaving the unsupported cloud to spread out sideways under its own weight. Some of the cloud was white, but other parts were dark patches of dirt and ash. The sight provoked my uncle's scientific instinct to see it from closer at hand. He ordered a boat to be got ready. He offered me the chance to go with him, but I preferred to carrying on studying (in fact he had himself set a writing exercise).

As he left the house he was brought a letter from Tascius' wife Rectina, who was terrified by the impending danger. Her villa lay on the foothills of Vesuvius, and there was no escape except by boat. She begged him to rescue her. He changed his plans. What had started out as a quest for information now needed a greatness of spirit. He launched the warships and boarded himself, prospective assistance for more than just Rectina, because that beautiful shoreline was heavily populated. He rushed to where other people were escaping and carried straight on into danger. It seems he had no fear, because he described everything and the shape of that evil cloud, dictating what he saw.

By this time ash was falling onto the ships, getting hotter and denser as they went closer. Next came bits of pumice, and blackened rocks, charred and shattered by the fire. Then they were on the shore, blocked by debris from the mountain. My uncle hesitated for an instant wondering whether to turn back as the helmsman was urging him. 'Fortune favours the brave [Terence, *Phormio* 203],' he said, 'make for Pomponianus.' Pomponianus was cut off at Stabiae by the width of the bay (which gradually curves round a basin filled by the sea) so he was not yet in danger, though it was obvious he would be as the catastrophe spread.

Pomponianus had already loaded his belongings onto his ships before the danger arrived. He intended to set sail the moment the wind [holding the cloud back] changed. The same wind brought my uncle right in, and he embraced the frightened man reassuring and encouraging him. In order to lessen the other man's fear with his own composure he asked to be taken to the baths. He bathed and dined, cheerfully or at least looking as if he was (which is just as impressive).

In the meantime great sheets of flame were lighting up many parts of Vesuvius. The light and brightness were all the more vivid against the darkness of the night. My uncle put it about that the fires came from farmhouses whose owners had fled without extinguishing the hearth fires, in order to calm people's fears. Then he rested, and looked to all accounts as if he was actually asleep. People passing his door could hear him snoring, which was rather resonant because he was stoutly built. The ground outside his room was rising so high with the build-up of ash and stones that if he had stayed there any longer escape would have been impossible. He got up and came out, rejoining Pomponianus and all the others who could not sleep.

They discussed what to do, whether to stay under cover or chance the open air. The buildings were being shaken by a series of strong tremors, and seemed to be shaking all over the place as if they had been ripped from their foundations. But outside, there was danger from the rocks that were falling down, even though they were light and porous. Weighing up the dangers, they plumped for the outside. As far as my uncle was concerned, that was a rational decision. The others just went for the option that frightened them the least. They tied pillows onto their heads to protect them against the shower of rocks.

Everywhere else in the world it was daylight now, but here the darkness was darker and murkier than any night. But they had torches and other lights. He decided to go down to the shore to see if there was any possibility of escape by sea. But it was still too rough and dangerous. Resting on a sail he took one or two drinks from the cold water he had asked for. Then came a sulphurous smell, warning of the approaching flames, and then the flames themselves. That sent the others into flight and roused him to his feet. Supported by two slaves he stood and then collapsed without warning. My understanding is that he was choked by the thick fumes blocking his windpipe which was weak by nature and often inflamed. When daylight returned two days after he died, his body was found untouched, unharmed, and still fully-clothed. He looked more asleep than dead.

All this time my mother and I were at Misenum but this has no historical interest and you only asked for information about his death so I will stop here. But I will add one thing, namely, that I have written down everything I did and heard at the time while my memory was still fresh. You will use which bits are important because writing a letter and history are two different things, as is writing for a friend or the public. Farewell.

Pliny the Younger, *Letters* vi.20, to Cornelius Tacitus
Since the letter, which you asked me to write about the death of my uncle, has stimulated your curiosity to learn what terrors and dangers affected me while I remained at Misenum because I broke off just as my story started. 'Though my shocked soul recoils, my tongue shall tell' [*Aeneid* ii.12].

My uncle having left us, I spent such time as was left on my studies (it was on their account indeed that I had stopped behind), until it was time for my bath. After that I had supper, and then fell into a brief and restless sleep. For several days earth tremors had been noticed but they didn't worry us much because that's quite normal in Campania. But they were so violent that night that everything around us seemed to be knocked over, not just shaken. My mother came rushing into my room, where she came across me getting up to wake her. We sat down in the forecourt of the house, which lay in a small place between the house and the sea. At the time I was still only seventeen. I don't know whether my behaviour at that precarious moment was courageous or foolhardy, but I picked up a copy of Livy and amused myself by browsing through his pages and even making extracts as I went just as if I was enjoying my usual leisure.

At that moment a friend of my uncle's who had recently joined him from Spain came up to us. Noticing me sitting beside my mother, and holding a book, he chided me for being so stupid and her for allowing me to be so. Even so, I carried on with my book. Though by now it was morning, the light was dim and faint. Buildings around us were on the point of collapsing and even though we were in open ground, it was too narrow and confined for us to stay there without imminent danger so we decided to leave the town. We were followed by a panic-stricken crowd (because to people driven demented by terror, any other prospect seems more sensible than what they come up with themselves), who shovelled us along as we came out by pushing hard behind us en masse.

Once we were beyond the houses we stopped, frozen, in the middle of a dangerous and terrifying scene. The carriages we had ordered brought out began running in different directions, even though the ground was flat, so that we could not steady them, even using large stones to chock them. The sea seemed to be sucked away and forced back by the earthquake. What is beyond doubt is that it left a much enlarged shoreline and many marine animals were left high and dry. On the other side, a terrible black cloud, fragmented by swift and jagged flashes, revealed various shapeless sheets of flame behind it. They were like sheet lightning but much bigger. At this point our Spanish friend spoke up, even more anxiously, 'If your brother, your uncle, is still alive, he will want you both to come out of this alive. If he's dead, he would want you to survive him, so don't hesitate to escape!' Our response was that we were unconcerned about our safety so long as his was in question. He didn't wait any longer and raced off to hurry out of the danger area as quickly as he could.

Not long after this, the cloud sank down to the surface and obscured the sea. Already it had blotted out Capri and the Misenum promontory. My mother begged, implored and ordered me to escape however I could. A youth could get away, but she was slow and old and would die in peace if she knew she hadn't caused my death as well. I said that I would not escape without her and gripped her hand to pull her along more quickly. Reluctantly she agreed, but blamed herself for being the cause of slowing me down.

By now ashes were falling but not thickly yet. I looked about: a thick black cloud was approaching from behind, covering the land like flood-water. I said, 'Let's get off the road while we can see where we are going otherwise we'll be knocked over and crushed by the crowd behind in the dark.' No sooner had we sat down to rest when it got dark. This wasn't the dark of a moonless or a cloudy night, but like the darkness in a closed room when the light is extinguished. Women could be heard screaming, babies crying, and men shouting. Some were calling for their parents, others for their children, or their husbands and trying to recognize each other from the voices that responded. People were bemoaning their fate, or that of their family. Some wanted to die to escape the terror of dying. Some raised their hands up to the gods but most were now sure there were no gods at all and that this was the final night at the end of the world.

Amongst these voices were some who made the real terror worse by imagining or inventing things. I recall that some said part of Misenum had collapsed, and another said it was ablaze. This wasn't true but they found some people who believed them. Some light returned now, which we thought meant a large burst of flames was approaching (as it turned out to be) rather than the restoration of daylight. However, the fire stayed some way from us so once again we were immersed in thick darkness. A heavy shower of ashes rained down on us, which we had every now and then to stand up to shake off, otherwise we would have been crushed and buried in the heap.

I could boast that, during all this scene of horror, not one groan, or expression of fear, escaped from me, had it not been for the fact that my miserable consolation lay in the thought that the whole human race was suffering the same calamity and that I was going to die with the world itself. Finally the darkness began to clear by increments, like a cloud or smoke. The real daylight returned and even the sun shone through but with a pallid light as it does when an eclipse is beginning. We were terrified by the sight of everything different, covered with deep ashes like a snowdrift. We went back to Misenum, where we refreshed ourselves as best we could and spent the night in anxiety and fear. It was mostly the latter because the earthquakes carried on while many terrified people ran up and down making their own tragedies and those of their friends seem ridiculous in comparison to what they were predicting would follow. However, neither of us had any intention of leaving, despite the dangers we had experienced and which still threatened us, until we heard what had happened to my uncle.

Naturally, these details aren't of any use to history and you will look at them with no concern for recording them. If they seem barely worth the trouble of putting in a letter, it is your fault for asking for them.

Pliny the Younger, *Letters* iii.6, to Annius Severus – Pliny wants a statue base inscribed with his name for a statue he has bought and wants to place in a temple
Out of a legacy which I have come in for I have just bought a Corinthian bronze, small it is true, but a charming and sharply-cut piece of work, so far as I have any knowledge of art, and that, as in everything else perhaps, is very slight. But as for the statue in question even I can appreciate its merits. For it is a nude, and neither conceals its faults, if there are any, nor hides at all its strong points. It represents an old man in a standing posture; the bones, muscles, nerves, veins, and even the wrinkles appear quite life-like; the hair is thin and scanty on the forehead; the brow is broad; the face wizened; the neck thin; the shoulders are bowed; the breast is flat, and the belly hollow. The back too gives the same impression of age, as

far as a back view can. The bronze itself, judging by the genuine colour, is old and of great antiquity. In fact, in every respect it is a work calculated to catch the eye of a connoisseur and to delight the eye of an amateur, and this is what tempted me to purchase it, although I am the merest novice.

But I bought it not to keep it at home – for as yet I have no Corinthian art work in my house – but that I might put it up in my native country in some frequented place, and I specially had in mind the Temple of Jupiter. For the statue seems to me to be worthy of the temple, and the gift to be worthy of the god. So I hope that you will show me your usual kindness when I give you a commission, and that you will undertake the following for me. Will you order a pedestal to be made, of any marble you like, to be inscribed with my name and titles, if you think the latter ought to be mentioned? I will send you the statue as soon as I can find any one who is not overburdened with luggage, or I will bring myself along with it, as I dare say you would prefer me to do. For, if only my duties allow me, I am intending to run down thither. You are glad that I promise to come, but you will frown when I add that I can only stay a few days. For the business which hitherto has kept me from getting away will not allow of my being absent any longer. Farewell.

Vitruvius, *De Architectura* vi.5 – Vitruvius, the Roman architect, describes how a Roman house should be designed and laid out

1. Once the positions of the rooms have been settled with respect to the parts of the sky, we must next consider how the rooms in private houses for the householders themselves, and those which are to be shared with visitors, should be laid out. Private rooms are the ones which no one has a right to enter uninvited, for example bedrooms (*cubicula*), dining rooms (*triclinia*), bathrooms (*balneae*) and others used for similar reasons. Communal rooms are those which any people can enter, even uninvited, for example vestibules (*vestibulae*), courtyards (*cava aedium*), peristyles (*peristylia*), and those which are used for the same purposes. Therefore it is unnecessary for persons of ordinary means to have magnificent vestibules, alcoves (*tabulinae*), and halls (*atria*), because such men fulfil their social obligations by visiting others, rather than being visited themselves.

2. Those whose business is country produce must have cattle stalls (*stabulae*) and shops (*tabernae*) in the entrance court, with crypts (*cryptae*), granaries (*horrea*), and store rooms (*apothecae*) which are intended to keep the produce in good condition rather than creating an elegant effect. Houses of bankers and tax officials need to be more spacious and impressive and protected against robbery, those of lawyers and public

speakers distinguished and spacious enough to accommodate meetings. For men of rank who hold office and magistracies, who have obligations to the community, regal vestibules, highly distinguished halls and peristyles, trees and wide avenues finished to a proper level of grandeur. Also, libraries, basilicas in a not dissimilar fashion to public buildings because public judgments as well as private trials and sentences are often held in such houses.

3. So, if houses are designed in a manner to suit different social classes, as described in the first book under 'Décor' [i.2.5], there will be nothing to criticise for the rules are suitable and correct in all circumstances. The rules hold not only in town, but also the country, except that in town the halls (*atria*) are usually next to the entrance (*ianua*) whereas in the country the peristyles come first, followed by the halls (*atria*) surrounded by paved colonnades looking over the palaestra and avenues.

Selected Inscriptions

(a) Tomb of Aulus Umbricius Scaurus junior (Pompeii *CIL* X.1024, *ILS* 6366, CC F91)

To Aulus Umbricius Scaurus, son of Aulus, of the Menenian tribe, *duumvir* with judicial power. The town councillors voted him a site for his monument, 2,000 sesterces for his funeral, and an equestrian statue to be set up in the Forum. His father Scaurus dedicated this to his son.

(b) Aulus Umbricius Scaurus senior (Pompeii *AE* (1992) 278a-d, CC H20b)

Scaurus' best mackerel sauce from the workshop of Scaurus. Best fish purée. Scaurus' best mackerel sauce. Finest fish purée from the workshop of Scaurus.

(c) Temple of Isis – dedication of a statue of Bacchus (Pompeii *CIL* X.847, CC E4)

Numerius Popidius Ampliatus, father, at his own expense

(d) Temple of Isis – dedication of a statue of Isis (Pompeii *CIL* X.849 CC E5)

Lucius Caecilius Phoebus erected this statue in a place given by the decurions

(e) Temple of Isis – rebuilt (Pompeii *CIL* X.846, *ILS* 6367, CC C5)

Numerius Popdius Celsinus, son of Numerius, restored from the foundations at his own expense the Temple of Isis, which had collapsed from an earth tremor. Although he was only six years old the councillors elected him one of them without any further fee because of his generosity.

(f) The Amphitheatre (Pompeii *CIL* X.852, *ILS* 5627, CC B9)

Gaius Quinctius Valgus, son of Gaius, and Marcus Porcius, son of Marcus, quinquennial *duoviri*, for the sake of the colony's honour built the place of spectacles [i.e. the amphitheatre] at their own expense and gave the place in perpetuity to the colonists.

(g) Marcus Nonius Balbus' tomb inscription (Herculaneum *AE* (1976), no. 144)

Since, on the grounds which Marcus Ofillius Celer, *duumvir* for the second time, put forth in his speech, it was in keeping with the dignity of our town to answer to the good deeds of Marcus Nonius Balbus, they resolved on this matter as follows: since Marcus Nonius Balbus, while he lived in this place, showed towards us individually and collectively the spirit of a father with many generosities, it was agreeable to the decurions that an equestrian statue of him should be placed in as busy a location as possible at public expense, and inscribed as follows: 'To Marcus Nonius Balbus, son of Marcus, of the voting tribe Menenia, praetor with proconsular power, patron, the entire council of the people of Herculaneum [set it up] on account of his merits.' Likewise, they resolved that in that place where his ashes were gathered a marble altar should be made and set up, and inscribed as follows at public expense: 'To Marcus Nonius Balbus, son of Marcus,' and that from that place the procession of the Parentalia should be led out and that it should be declared that one day be celebrated in his honour out of the gymnastic games which are usually held, and that when in the theatre shows are celebrated his honorific seat should be laid out.

(h) Claudius' harbour works at Ostia (*Thylander* B310) AD 47

Tiberius Claudius Caesar Augustus Germanicus, son of Drusus, Pontifex Maximus [i.e. Chief Priest], holding tribunician power for the 6th time, designated consul for the 4th time, hailed as imperator 12 times, Father of his Country, freed the City [i.e. Rome] from the danger of floods with trenches drawn from the Tiber for the sake of the harbour works and sent [the water] out into the sea.

Abbreviations and Suggestions for Further Study

AE = *L'Annee épigraphique* (Paris, 1888-).
CC = Cooley and Cooley 2004.
CIL = *Corpus Inscriptionum Latinorum* (Berlin, 1863-) in 16 volumes.
ILS = Dessau, H., 1892-1916 *Inscriptionum Latinae Selectae*, Berlin (3 volumes).

There are numerous books concerned with Pompeii, many of which are recent, up-to-date and extremely well-illustrated with detailed plans and photographs. Unfortunately both Herculaneum and Ostia are very much less well-served, apart of course from scholarly publications of excavations but these are beyond the scope of the average student and are confined to specialist libraries. In Herculaneum's case this is understandable; only a small part of the town has been exposed, and far less is known about it. Ostia is more of a mystery. The site has been extensively explored and it is both easily reached from Rome and a very popular destination for visitors on classical tours. However, the standard work in English on Ostia (by Russell Meiggs) was written over half a century ago, has very limited illustrations and is both difficult and expensive to come by. Some of the books listed below do consider the houses at Herculaneum and Ostia as well as those at Pompeii, but there is no equivalent treatment for the public buildings in all three places.

Allison, P.M., *The Insula of the Menander at Pompeii*, volume III: *The Finds, A Contextual Study* (Oxford, Clarendon Press 2006).

Beard, M., *Pompeii: The Life of a Roman Town* (London, Profile Books 2008) – a lively modern account of city life.

Berry, J., *Unpeeling Pompeii* (Milan, Electa 1998).

Berry, J., *The Complete Pompeii* (London, Thames and Hudson 2007) – a superbly illustrated account of Pompeii, with a number of references to Herculaneum.

Butterworth, A. and Laurence, R., *Pompeii: The Living City* (London, Weidenfield and Nicolson 2005).

Calza, G. and Becatti, G., *Ostia* (Rome, Istituto Poligrafico 2008, revised by M. Floriani Squarciapino) – the site guidebook, now dating back several decades.

Capasso, G., *Journey to Pompeii* (Ottaviano, Capware 2005).

Clarke, J.R., *The Houses of Roman Italy, 100 BC-AD 250: Ritual, Space and Decoration* (Berkeley and Los Angeles, University of California 1991).

Connolly, P., *Pompeii* (London, Macdonald Educational 1979).

Cooley, A. and Cooley, M.G.L., *Pompeii. A Sourcebook* (London, Routledge 2004).

de Caro, S., *Il Santuario di Iside* (Naples, Electa, 2006) (Temple of Isis).

Deiss, J., *Herculaneum* (New York, Crowell 1966) – a comprehensive review of Herculaneum's life and history, but now very outdated and with some significant inaccuracies.

Dobbins, J.J. and Foss, P.W. (eds), *The World of Pompeii* (London, Routledge 2007) – an invaluable collection of essays covering the latest research on Pompeii.

Franklin, J.L. *Pompeii Difficile Est* (Ann Arbor, University of Michigan Press 2001).

Grant, M.R., *Cities of Vesuvius* (New York, Macmillan 1971).

Guidobaldi, M.P., *Ercolano: Guide to the Site* (Naples, Electa 2006).

Guzzo, P.G. and d'Ambrosio, A., *Pompeii: Guide to the Site* (Naples, Electa 2002).

Hermansen, G., *Ostia: Aspects of Roman City Life* (University of Alberta 1981).

Hope, V.M., *Death in Ancient Rome: A Sourcebook.* (London, Routledge 2007).

Hope, V.M., 'Status and Identity in the Roman World' in in Huskisson, J. (ed.), *Experiencing Rome: Culture, Identity and Power in the Roman Empire* (London, Routledge 2000), pp. 125-52.

Keppie, L., *Understanding Roman Inscriptions* (London, Batsford 1991).

Laurence, R., *Roman Pompeii: Space and Society* (Abingdon, Routledge 2007).

Ling, R., *Pompeii: History, Life and Afterlife* (Stroud, Tempus 2005).

Ling, R., *The Insula of the Menander at Pompeii*, volume I: *The Structures* (Oxford, Clarendon Press 1997).

Ling, R. and Ling, L., *The Insula of the Menander at Pompeii*, volume II: *The Decorations* (Oxford, Clarendon Press 2005).

Maiuri, A., *Herculaneum* (Rome, Istituto Poligrafico 1977).

Meiggs, R., *Roman Ostia* (Oxford, Clarendon Press 1960).

Moeller, W., *The Wool Trade of Ancient Pompeii* (Leiden, Brill 1976).

Panetta, M.R., *Pompeii: The History, Life and Art of the Buried City* (White Star, Vercelli 2004) – a truly sumptuous large format colour book containing invaluable aerial images and photographs of buildings, finds and decoration.

Richardson, L., *Pompeii: An Architectural History* (Baltimore, John Hopkins University Press 1988).

Rickman, G., *Roman Granaries and Store Buildings* (Cambridge, Cambridge University Press 1971)

Wallace-Hadrill, A.W., *Houses and Society in Pompeii and Herculaneum* (Princeton, Princeton University Press 1994).

Ward-Perkins, J.B., *Roman Architecture* (London, Faber and Faber 1988).

Ward-Perkins, J.B. and Claridge, A., *Pompeii AD 79* (London, Imperial Tobacco 1976) – guidebook to the London exhibition held in 1976.

Online resources

Internet resources for Pompeii, Herculaneum and Ostia are increasing all the time. Weblinks are prone to change without notice, but at the time of writing the following were particularly useful:

General

www.romanbritain.freeserve.co.uk/cc6reading.htm – specifically designed to support A-level and university studies of the three cities, this site includes a large number of links to buildings and aspects of all three cities mentioned in this book.

www.youtube.com – a general search under each city name will yield results, but a search under KSHSClassCiv will produce links to films taken in individual buildings at all three sites.

Pompeii

www.pompeiiinpictures.com/pompeiiinpictures/ – an immensely useful site with pictures of practically every building reached via clickable maps and an index of names.

http://www.pompeiisites.org/ – home page of the Soprintendenza of Pompeii.

Herculaneum

http://www.herculaneum.org/ – home page of the Herculaneum Conservation Project.

http://www.proxima-veritati.auckland.ac.nz/Herculaneum/ – a virtual tour of the site.

Ostia

http://www.ostia-antica.org/dict.htm – this superbly comprehensive site
has clickable plans taking the visitor to all the buildings, and pages
with plans and discussions of each.

Ostia, Building of Serapis, entrance area. This imposing and well-preserved
structure, dating to the Hadrianic period, had apartments on upper floors and
shops on lower floors. A shrine to Serapis was added in the early third century.
The complex was connected to an adjacent public baths.

Index

This is a select index. Pompeii, Herculaneum and Ostia are constantly mentioned throughout the text. Names are indicated by their most commonly known form. Numbers in **bold** indicate pages with illustrations.

CLASSICAL WORLD SERIES

RECENT TITLES IN THE SERIES
(for a full list see opposite title page)

Roman Frontiers in Britain
David J. Breeze

ISBN 978 1 85399 698 6

Hadrian's Wall and the Antonine Wall defined the far northern limits of the Roman Empire in Britain. Today, the spectacular remains of these great frontier works stand as mute testimony to one of the greatest empires the world has ever seen. This new accessible account, illustrated with 25 detailed photographs, maps and plans, describes the building of the Walls and reconstructs what life was like on the frontier. It places the Walls into their context both in Britain and in Europe, examining the development of Roman frontier installations over four centuries.

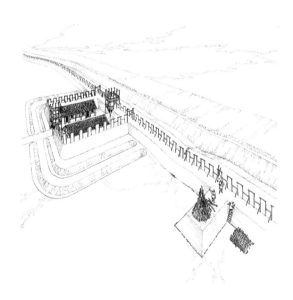

Greek Literature in the Roman Empire
Jason König

ISBN 978 1 85388 713 6

In this book Jason König offers for the first time an accessible yet comprehensive account of the multi-faceted Greek literature of the Roman Empire, focusing especially on the first three centuries AD. He covers in turn the Greek novels of this period, the satirical writing of Lucian, rhetoric, philosophy, scientific and miscellanistic writing, geography and history, biography and poetry, providing a vivid introduction to key texts with extensive quotation in translation. He also looks beyond the most commonly studied authors to reveal the full richness of this period's literature. The challenges and pleasures these texts offer to their readers have come to be newly appreciated in the classical scholarship of the last two or three decades. In addition there has been renewed interest in the role played by novelistic and rhetorical writing in the Greek culture of the Roman Empire more broadly, and in the many different ways in which these texts respond to the world around them. This volume offers a broad introduction to those exciting developments.

Early Greek Lawgivers
John David Lewis

ISBN 978 1 85399 697 9

Early Greek Lawgivers examines the men who brought laws to the early Greek city states, as an introduction both to the development of law and to basic issues in early legal practice. The lawgiver was a man of special status, who could resolve disputes without violence and bring a sense of order to his community by proposing comprehensive norms of ethical conduct. He established those norms in the form of oral or written laws. Crete, under king Minos, became an example of the ideal community for later Greeks, such as Plato. The unwritten laws of Lycurgus established the foundations of the Spartan state, in contrast with the written laws of Solon in Athens. Other lawgivers illustrate particular issues in early law; for instance, Zaleucus on the divine source of laws; Philolaus on family law; Phaleas on communism of property; and Hippodamus on civic planning.

Greek Vases: An Introduction
Elizabeth Moignard

ISBN 978 1 85399 691 7

Greek Vases is an introduction to the painted vases which were an ever-present but understated feature of life in the Greek world between the end of the Bronze Age and the rise of Rome, and, in the modern world, an important component of museum collections since the eighteenth century. The book uses specific illustrated examples to explore the archaeological use of vases as chronological indicators, the use of the various shapes, their scenes of myth and everyday life and what these tell us, the way in which we think about their makers, and how they are treated today as museum objects and archaeological evidence.

Key features of the text include a brief accessible introduction to the vases with school and university students in mind, discussion of the different approaches to vases adopted by their very different groups of users, and an approach designed to help viewers understand how to look at these fascinating objects for themselves.

Athletics in the Ancient World
Zahra Newby

ISBN 978 1 85399 688 7

The athletic competitions that took place during festivals such as that at Olympia, or within the confines of city gymnasia, were a key feature of life in ancient Greece. From the commemoration of victorious athletes in poetry or sculpture to the archaeological remains of baths, gymnasia and stadia, surviving evidence offers plentiful testimony to the importance of athletic activity in Greek culture, and its survival well into Roman times.

This book offers an introduction to the many forms that athletics took in the ancient world, and to the sources of evidence by which we can study it. As well as looking at the role of athletics in archaic and classical Greece, it also covers the less-explored periods of the Hellenistic and Roman worlds. Many different aspects of athletics are considered – not only the well-known contests of athletic festivals, but also the place of athletic training within civic education and military training, and its integration into the bathing culture of the Roman world.